"Deepak Reju writes with conviction and compassion about the sobering reality of child abuse and the challenge of protecting children in this fallen world. Highlighting both the responsibility and privilege of our stewardship, Deepak's straightforward, thorough, and well-researched insights will instill in any parent or church leader a healthy fear and God-dependent confidence while providing us with practical steps and effective strategies for fulfilling the calling and responsibility we have as God's stewards. We earnestly encourage church leaders to embrace Deepak's concern and apply his counsel for the protection and the joy of the next generation."

Pastor David and Sally Michael, Founders, Children Desiring God

"Child sexual abuse in the church is a scandal and yet many of us in church are woefully ill-equipped to identify danger signs, understand our legal responsibilities, or respond in an appropriate pastoral manner to the victims. In this timely book, Deepak Reju addresses all of these areas of concern, offering helpful advice to pastors, elders, and Christians in general on what the reality of this evil requires of them in terms of organization, wisdom, and action. Whether your church is just starting to formulate a child protection policy or seeking to protect the children in its care more effectively, this book will be a very useful resource in addressing the challenges and, most important of all, in keeping children safe and giving comfort and care to the victims of abuse."

Carl R. Trueman, Pastor, Cornerstone Presbyterian Church, Ambler, PA; Paul Woolley Professor of Church History, Westminster Theological Seminary, Philadelphia

"Deepak has given the church a fine gift. He has written a very practical plan for churches so we can better love and protect our children and teens. It won't overburden a church with endless regulations, but it will give church leadership what they must know, and it will lay out what church leadership must teach its members and ministry staff. This book will, guaranteed, make you and your church wiser."

Ed Welch, Author and CCEF Faculty

"Everyone agrees that we should be on guard to protect children in our churches. What's been lacking is a clear and concise guide that shows church leaders how. In *On Guard*, Deepak Reju has now provided us with a theologically grounded and deeply practical guide precisely for this purpose."

Timothy Paul Jones, PhD, C. Edwin Gheens Professor of Christian Family Ministry at The Southern Baptist Theological Seminary

"*On Guard* is a road map that will help your church, its leaders, staff and congregation create a safer environment for families. It does not pull its punches delivering case studies, facts, and figures that will shock many, and by deconstructing the stereotypical image of the sexual predator, it forces the reader to reflect on the reality that predators very often hide in plain sight, behind the facade of the all-American father, youth pastor, preacher, or highly respected member of the congregation. If your church hasn't got a child protection policy or you want to test the one you have, this provides all the references and checklists you will need. Whether inside or outside the church, this is a must-read for all child protection professionals."

Jim Gamble QPM, CEO INEQE Safe & Secure; former CEO of the Child Exploitation and Online Protection (CEOP) Centre; founding Chair of the Virtual Global Taskforce on Child Protection; lead on Association of Chief Police Officers (ACPO) Child Abuse Investigation until 2011

"How should a church respond to a convicted sex offender who, after serving his sentence, wants to join your church? How do we affirm the gospel of grace without making naïve and tragic mistakes? How can predators be identified and what 'best practices' do we need to guard against abuse within the church, even by leaders? Sad to say, we really need this book."

Michael Horton, Professor of Theology, Westminster Seminary California; cohost of the White Horse Inn

"The church has been woefully behind the curve when it comes to addressing sexual abuse. Fortunately, *On Guard* by Deepak Reju brings a much needed resource to church leadership. Reju is a shepherd who clearly loves the vulnerable sheep. Beyond statistics and stories, Reju speaks into the heart of contemporary church life with insight that faces evil and also brings practical help. I recommend every new pastor or intern read this book. *On Guard: Preventing and Responding to Child Abuse at Church* is a mouthful we're going to have to digest to move toward the front of the curve."

Andrew J. Schmutzer, PhD, Professor of Biblical Studies, Moody Bible Institute; author/editor of *The Long Journey Home: Understanding and Ministering to the Sexually Abused*

"*On Guard* is a much-needed bomb and balm. It detonates many dangerous assumptions of the evangelical church regarding child abuse, and it points us toward true healing and wise safety measures. This is a must-read for every pastor and ministry leader and a gift of love to every child. I wish this book had been published decades ago!"

Peter Hubbard, Teaching Pastor, North Hills Community Church, Taylors, SC; author of *Love Into Light*

"Thanks to *On Guard*, many children will be protected from the horrors of child abuse. In addition to providing a more comprehensive approach toward child abuse, he offers helpful strategies to prevent and respond to abuse at church. All pastors, children ministry leaders, church staff, and parents need Deepak's book."

> **Justin S. Holcomb,** Episcopal priest; seminary professor; coauthor of *Rid of My Disgrace*

"I can't recommend Deepak's book highly enough. Deepak provides a thorough education on child protection for your childcare workers, practical help in implementing a child protection policy at your church, and sets an appropriately tough standard that will scare the daylights out of any predators looking to target your children. Get a case of these books to give to your children's ministry workers as a training tool to equip them in their service and care of your children."

> **Marty Machowski,** Children's Pastor; author of *The Gospel Story Bible* and *Gospel Story* curriculum, *Long Story Short*, and *Old Story New*

"This book is a must-read for every church and pastor. The church has a moral responsibility to be fully equipped in the protection of children under its care and how to respond in a God-honoring way when our best efforts at prevention fail. We have not lived up to this standard, but Deepak has served the church well by writing this needed resource. It is now our responsibility to study it, examine our current practices at each church, and make necessary changes. Make sure every church and pastor you know gets a copy."

> **Brad Hambrick,** Pastor of Counseling at The Summit Church, Durham, NC (www.bradhambrick.com/beyondprevention/)

"I know of no single book that captures well the full picture and essential need to protect children in the modern church and how to accomplish it wisely . . . until now. I am deeply grateful that Deepak Reju wrote this book. His wise pastor's heart and years of credible experience he brings to this area of ministry permeates from every page. *On Guard* is thoroughly biblical and immensely practical. Every pastor, church leader, and church member working with children in the local church must read this book. This is one of the most important books for the local church I have read in many years!"

> **Brian Croft,** Senior Pastor, Auburndale Baptist Church; founder, Practical Shepherding; author

"*On Guard: Preventing and Responding to Child Abuse at Church* needs to be in the hands of every pastor and ministry leader in every church. This candid, compassionate, and comprehensive manual provides exactly what the church desperately needs to protect children and to protect the reputation of Christ and the Bride of Christ. Replete with wise biblical principles and practical real-life policies and procedures, *On Guard* equips the church to take the lead in proactively protecting the most precious and vulnerable among us."

    Bob Kellemen, PhD, Executive Director, Biblical Counseling Coalition; author of *Gospel-Centered Counseling*

"Rev. Reju boldly articulates that the church does not, in fact will not, write a child safety plan if it does not understand the call of Scripture as the basis for such a plan. From chapter to chapter, the author extracts from numerous scripture verses and stories the sound theological foundation for a child safety plan. He emphasizes that every movement toward the development of a child safety plan must embrace our duty to love the church and the little ones in its care, but also to abhor the moral failure of doing nothing to protect little ones from harm or restricting potential abusers from unfettered access to do harm."

    Beth A. Swagman, MSW, ACSW, JD, Director of Safe Place Consulting, PLC, Grand Rapids, MI; author of *Preventing Child Abuse: Creating a Safe Place*

"Sexual predators target children in churches. This sobering truth ought to lead us to pray—and prepare. In his timely book, Deepak Reju helps pastors and parents consider what it means to proactively defend children from those who would seek to do them harm. This valuable resource brings needed sobriety along with practical wisdom to assist churches in developing policies, procedures, and response plans to help guard our children. I have great hope that God will use this book for his glory and the good of many children."

    Garrett Kell, Lead Pastor, Del Ray Baptist Church, Alexandria, VA

"*On Guard* provides a compelling and challenging glimpse into one of the gritty realities facing churches today—the prevalence of child sexual abuse. Reju's statistics and stories are startling. But his recommendations for a thorough child protection policy and suggestions for writing one are practical, helpful, and insightful—born from real-world experience. *On Guard* challenges churches, leaders, and parents to proactively protect the children in their care. A valuable resource for churches of all sizes!"

    Kathy Stout-LaBauve, LCSW, Vice President of Aftercare, International Justice Mission

"In a perfect world, a book like *On Guard* would not be necessary. But our world is broken, and we need serious help navigating the often complex issues of protection, justice, and healing when it comes to the most vulnerable in our churches. Deepak Reju has met this need in a clear, practical, and powerful way."

Jared C. Wilson, Pastor, Middletown Springs Community Church, Vermont; author of *The Wonder-Working God*

"I wish we lived in a world where books like *On Guard* were not necessary. Since we don't, however, I am very glad that Deepak Reju wrote this excellent book. *On Guard* is an immensely helpful guide for pastors and other church leaders who want to prevent and respond to child abuse in their midst. I recommend that you read it and implement its wisdom before you need it."

Mike McKinley, Pastor Sterling Park Baptist Church (Sterling, VA); author of *Am I Really a Christian?*

"A lead pastor often has his mind wrapped up in the next sermon, staff issues, the overall vision of the church, and shepherding the adults of his congregation well. But, how often does he stop to think about the critical logistical issues that could build or utterly destroy the health of a congregation, such as the physical safety of the children and youth in its ministries? And is he prepared to shepherd well when a horrible situation occurs involving a child? *On Guard* changed how I think. I have never disagreed with the principles and wisdom in the book, but nor have I really given much attention to them so I could lead and be accountable for our children's ministry staff. Deepak Reju has addressed the vital issues of safeguarding and responding to child abuse in the context of a local church within a theological and pastoral framework. Whether you are a children's ministry volunteer or a lead pastor, this is an essential read."

Jay Thomas, Lead Pastor, Chapel Hill Bible Church

"*On Guard* should be mandatory reading for every pastor! For too long, the sexual abuse of children has been one of the darkest places inside the Church. This is the reason I am so excited to endorse this book by Deepak Reju that helps to shine light and brings hope to this issue. Not only does this book do a thorough job in identifying the complex issues, but it also offers fantastic practical guidance on how to confront and address abuse in a manner that protects children and serves survivors."

Boz Tchividjian, Executive Director, GRACE (Godly Response to Abuse in the Christian Environment)

"This is a full book-length treatment of a terrifyingly common reality—the sexual abuse of children in religious environments. It is well-grounded in biblical and theological truth, and it provides concrete information both about the extent of the problem and about the specific steps that churches must take to address the problem (steps that are also directly relevant to synagogues and mosques). It should be required reading for the leaders of all religious communities."

> **Dr. Samuel Logan,** International Director of the World Reformed Fellowship

"We all might wish that a book like this wouldn't have to be written, but wishful thinking is exactly the kind of thing that puts children at risk. Child predators aim to victimize children, and they know that many churches are doing little to keep them out. Deepak Reju has done an enormous service to God's people by showing us how to keep our churches *On Guard* against child predators. This book is extremely practical and a must-read for pastors and church leaders."

> **Denny Burk**, Professor of Biblical Studies, The Southern Baptist Theological Seminary

"One of the greatest challenges facing the twenty-first century church in North America is how to protect our children from child abuse. While the moral responsibility to guard our children from emotional and physical harm is undisputed, it seems that too many church leaders continue to respond wrongly to allegations and even the proof that abuse has occurred. How to handle these situations becomes overwhelmingly confusing and complex when a church has not properly planned for how to prevent and respond to abuse. In *On Guard*, Deepak Reju has served us all. He pulls back the curtain of child abuse and provides a clear-headed analysis of the problem, and then he provides eleven strategies for preventing and responding to abuse. We can't get this wrong! The moral, physical, and emotional health of our children and the faithful witness of the justice and loving kindness of God displayed in the gospel depend on it."

> **Keith Whitfield, PhD,** Assistant Professor of Christian Theology, Southeastern Baptist Theological Seminary, Wake Forest, NC

"Authority exercised well is one of the most beautiful pictures we have of God and His character. Authority abused, especially among children, is one of the most heinous sins and offenses against God because it lies about his image and who he is. In *On Guard*, Deepak reflects pastorally, practically, and biblically on how to exercise authority well so that Christian leaders and parents can most effectively protect and care for children in the church. This is an essential resource for every local church, filling a much-needed gap and giving practical tools that will honor God, protect children, and strengthen the witness of the gospel in a dark, dark world."

Ryan Townsend, Executive Director, 9Marks

"Dr. Deepak Reju brings practical and pastoral wisdom to a subject not many people are willing to talk about today, despite the fact that one in three girls and one in four boys will be sexually abused at some point in their childhood. His eight strategies for protecting against abuse are worth the price of the book. Read this one and weep. Then get to work to protect our children."

C. Ben Mitchell, PhD, Provost, Vice President for Academic Affairs, and Graves Professor of Moral Philosophy, Union University

ON GUARD

. . . .

PREVENTING AND RESPONDING TO CHILD ABUSE AT CHURCH

. . . .

DEEPAK REJU

New
Growth
Press

www.newgrowthpress.com

New Growth Press, Greensboro, NC 27404
Copyright © 2014 by Deepak Reju

Cover Design: Faceout Books, faceoutstudio.com
Interior Design and Typesetting: Lisa Parnell, lparnell.com

ISBN: 978-1-939946-51-5 (Print)
ISBN: 978-1-939946-99-7 (eBook)

Library of Congress Cataloging-in-Publication Data
Reju, Deepak, 1969–
   On guard : preventing and responding to child abuse at church / Deepak Reju.
     pages cm
   ISBN 978-1-939946-51-5 — ISBN 978-1-939946-99-7 (ebook) 1. Church work with children. 2. Child abuse—Prevention. 3. Child abuse—Religious aspects—Christianity. I. Title.
   BV639.C4R45 2014
   261.8'3271—dc23
                                                                2014021835

Printed in the United States of America

21 20 19 18 17 16 15 14   2 3 4 5 6

Contents

· · · ·

Acknowledgments

I've often heard it said that writing a book is a labor of love. You pour yourself into it with the hope that it will help someone. *My first and foremost desire is that as a result of this book, children will be protected from the horrors of child abuse.*

My second desire for this book was to fill a gap. Everywhere I go, lawyers and psychologists are talking about child abuse and telling the church what to do, but pastors rarely have anything to say. I'm a pastor, and I spend a lot of time working alongside our children's ministry and youth staff. I wanted to make a statement as a pastor who labors on the "inside" of a church.

My third desire was to state what I thought would be a more comprehensive approach preventing and responding to child abuse at church. If you look at the literature on child abuse directed at churches, you see a lot about writing a policy, screening, reporting abuse, and responding to abuse. But there was very little other instruction, and what was available was often out of print. Hence, my eleven strategies to prevent and respond to abuse at church.

Thanks to Barbara Juliani and Marty Machowski, both of whom believed that this would be worthy of putting into print—and who took a risk on a relatively new author.

Thanks to the elder board and members of Capitol Hill Baptist Church (CHBC) and our very talented children's ministry team—especially Gio Lynch, Jennilee Miller, and Connie Dever. What a delight it is to work and serve at a church that makes the gospel so central to everything.

I'm grateful for Carl Simmons and Gretchen Logterman who worked through the manuscript with me and made this a better book. Thanks also to writer and reporter J.C. Derrick, who edited and gave me feedback on my very first draft, long before I had a publisher.

Thanks *especially* to my very dear wife, Sarah, who has shown great kindness to me for more than a decade, treating me much better than I deserve.

INTRODUCTION

· · · ·

WHY SHOULD YOU CARE?

Jonathan was shocked. A convicted sex offender had molested a young boy in the bathroom. The three deacons in the church were supposed to be watching him but let down their guard when it came time to collect the offering. As the new pastor, Jonathan didn't know what to do. No one had described anything like this in seminary.

In another church, Carl, the youth pastor, would typically drive the kids home after their Friday night meetings. Darla wasn't his first victim. He would often drop her off last and would "touch" her after the other kids were gone. Pats, tickles, and poking turned into caressing in inappropriate places.

Janel was an innocent teenager in a hallway of the local mega-church heading home after a youth event. Sam, a building manager, pulled her into an empty classroom and forced her to have sex. She was at the wrong place at the wrong time. No one else was around, and she didn't know what to do, so she just gave in to Sam's demands. He threatened her so that she wouldn't tell anyone, but it was hard to hide because she cried the whole rest of the day. Sam had a rap sheet. He had been hired because he had friends who worked for the church, and no one had bothered to check into his past.

You might be surprised that these situations actually happened in churches. Of all places, aren't churches supposed to be associated with good things—a loving God, sacrificial believers, children's choirs, and Christmas pageants? Take a brief look at the local news, or live long enough in a fallen world, and you'll quickly see how Satan makes his way into churches, wreaking havoc in all kinds of ways (1 Peter 5:8). Pastors have affairs; people embezzle money; Christians gossip, complain, and bicker with one another. And that's just the tip of the iceberg when it comes to what can go wrong in a local church.

In this book, we are dealing with one particular manifestation of evil—*wicked people doing unspeakable wrong against children.* Those who think that churches are immune from this problem are deeply mistaken. As we'll find in the pages ahead, some sexual offenders deliberately target churches because they want to take advantage of naive Christians. To deny that this could ever happen in a church puts our kids at risk. Denial doesn't get anyone anywhere in a fallen world filled with sin and evil.

As you read this book, my hope and prayer is that you'll grow in your understanding of the problem (including how child abusers act and think) and of ways to lower the risk of an offender harming children in your church. With that said, let's begin.

Section One

Getting Familiar with the Problem of Child Abuse

CHAPTER 1

. . . .

THE NATURE OF THE PROBLEM

In the movie *Grand Canyon,* Kevin Kline plays the role of an immigration lawyer who flees from a bumper-to-bumper traffic jam by heading down a side street. Within just a few minutes, a rather predictable Hollywood scenario unfolds: An upper-class lawyer driving a fancy car stalls in a dangerous neighborhood. He calls for a tow truck, but while he waits, a street gang surrounds his car and starts threatening him.

The tow truck soon arrives, and the old driver starts to hook up the disabled car, much to the chagrin of the gang members. "What are you doing, old man? Can't you see you are spoiling our fun?" protests the gang leader.

Taking him aside, the driver explains, "Man, the world ain't supposed to work like this. Maybe you don't know that, but this ain't the way it's supposed to be. I'm supposed to be able to do my job without askin' you if I can. And the dude is supposed to be able to wait with his car without you rippin' him off. Everything's supposed to be different than what it is here."

Welcome to the cold, hard reality of life in a corrupt and sinful world.[1]

Not the Way It's Supposed to Be

In the beginning, it wasn't this way. God made the world, and everything he made, even the first man and woman, he deemed "good" (Genesis 1:5, 12, 18, 21, 25, 31). But quickly things went wrong as Adam and Eve chose to listen to the words of the serpent rather than trust in God (Genesis 3:1–13). Sin entered the world through the first couple and has been passed on to every generation since then.

The Bible explains to us why this world is not the way it is supposed to be—sin entered the world and corrupted everything. That's right—*everything*. No one and nothing escapes its evil grasp. The apostle Paul wrote, "There is no one righteous, not even one; there is no one who understands; there is no one who seeks God. . . . For all have sinned and fall short of the glory of God" (Romans 3:10–11, 23).

Every human being is a sinner. No one escapes the curse of Genesis 3. Sin has corrupted every part of our human existence—our thinking, our actions, our desires, our plans, our hopes, and our dreams. Our nature is sinful from birth (Psalm 51:5). Every bit of who we are is affected.

It is no surprise, then, that some adults will do unspeakably wrong things to children. In a fallen world, one sees and experiences all kinds of evil. Some men and women are so distorted by sin that they willingly commit atrocious acts against innocent children. I am going to call these people by a variety of terms—sex offender, child abuser, or perpetrator. Sometimes I will even call them *sexual predators* because that's exactly what they are—evil people who deliberately prey on kids.

Abuse and Moral Authority

Child abuse can be defined as any act or failure to act resulting in imminent risk, serious injury, death, physical or emotional or sexual harm, or exploitation of a child.

God has entrusted the care of children to parents (and extended family), which means they have the moral responsibility to protect, feed, mentor, care for, and love their children. There is also a more general sense in which God has given moral responsibility to adults. Church members care for other people's kids in children's ministry; teachers guide children through their education; community baseball and soccer coaches encourage and equip kids with skills in a particular sport. Even an adult passing by a child lying hurt in the street will feel more than just the tug of a good Samaritan; he will feel a natural impulse to help someone who is weaker and more vulnerable than himself.

God has given parents a unique authority over their children, but in some sense, he has given any adult who watches over a child—a teacher, coach, babysitter, or even a fellow church member—a level of responsibility and authority for that child. Every good authority reflects God; and every bad authority speaks a lie to children about God and who he is. When any adult—relative or otherwise—abuses a child, it is a violation of the moral authority entrusted to adults. Abuse is antithetical to an adult's God-given charge to care for kids. To put it more bluntly: Abuse in any form is *wrong*. There is *never* an excuse to abuse a child.

Show Me the Numbers

To get a greater sense of the problem, a quick statistical overview of child abuse is helpful:

- There are approximately 747,000 registered sex offenders in the U.S. alone.[2]
- There are more than 100,000 sexual offenders who fail to report every year.[3]
- As many as one in three girls and one in four boys will be sexually abused at some point in their childhood.[4]
- Approximately thirty percent of all cases are reported to authorities—meaning that seventy percent never get proper attention or prosecution.[5]

- Over 63,000 cases of child sexual abuse were reported in 2010.[6]
- Offenders typically prey on children they know, not strangers. Most perpetrators are acquaintances, but as many as forty-seven percent are family or extended family.[7]
- Almost half (forty-seven percent) of the offenders who sexually assaulted victims under age six were family members, compared with forty-two percent of whom assaulted youth ages six through eleven, and twenty-four percent of whom assaulted juveniles ages twelve through seventeen.[8]
- The Department of Justice reports that children under age twelve make up half of all victims of forced sodomy, forced fondling, or sexual assault with an object.[9]
- Numerous experts have made it clear that sexual predators often have not just one or two victims, but dozens. The Abel and Harlow Child Molestation Prevention Study found that each child molester averages twelve child victims and seventy-one acts of molestation. An earlier study by Dr. Gene Abel found that out of 561 sexual offenders interviewed there were more than 291,000 incidents involving more than 195,000 total victims. This same study found that only three percent of these sexual offenders have a chance of getting caught.[10]
- A 2007 FBI report states the following:
  - One out of five girls will be sexually molested before her eighteenth birthday;
  - One out of six boys will be sexually molested before his eighteenth birthday;
  - One out of every seven victims of sexual assault reported to law enforcement agencies was under age six; and
  - Forty percent of the offenders who victimized children under age six were juveniles (under eighteen).[11]

Appalling, isn't it? A quick glance at the numbers shows how pervasive the problem is. This fills out the Bible's picture of sin with more specifics, helping us to see how common sexual and physical abuse is in our society.

When the Church Fails Our Kids

While there are no statistical reports on child abusers in churches, experts have collected a slew of anecdotes about offenders who deliberately target churches. If you think it can't happen at your church, then be forewarned: it can.

Anna Salter, one of the nation's experts on sexual abuse, describes the life of Mr. Raines. Here is his story, in his own words:

> I want to describe a child molester I know very well. This man was raised by devout Christian parents. As a child he rarely missed church. Even after he became an adult, he was faithful as a church member. He was a straight-A student in high school and college. He has been married and has a child of his own. He coached Little League baseball. He was a choir director at his church. He never used any illegal drugs. He never had a drink of alcohol. He was a clean-cut, all-American boy. Everyone seemed to like him. He was a volunteer in numerous civic community functions. He had a well-paying career job. He was considered "well-to-do" in society. But from the age of thirteen years old, he sexually molested little boys. He never victimized a stranger. All of his victims were friends.... I know this child molester very well because it is me.[12]

Mr. Raines has been out on parole on several occasions—and scary enough, tries to infiltrate churches to become, of all things, a volunteer children's choir director. He does this despite the fact that he has had at least two incarcerations and three criminal convictions for child molestation.

How is this possible, you say? Mr. Raines is a very likable fellow, so his previous churches quickly grew to trust him. And once those

Christians trusted him, Mr. Raines put himself in direct contact with as many kids as possible. What better way to have access to kids than to be their choir director?

Sexual offenders are not dumb. They are deliberate and calculating. The very thing Christians see as strengths—love for others, a trusting disposition—perpetrators see as weaknesses on which they can prey. Dr. Salter writes: "I believe in my heart the next time Mr. Raines gets out of prison, he will successfully ingratiate himself in youth activities in a church once more. He will do this even though he now has at least three criminal convictions for child molestation and likely more, all of which any church could have discovered. But who will check criminal records for such an outstanding, polite, well-spoken young man? After all, volunteers are hard to come by."[13]

Many perpetrators know that churches are struggling to find volunteers to help in children's ministry, and they want to exploit that fact fully. I recently sat down with a pastor, his children's minister, and their lead volunteers. Only five to ten percent of their church membership was willing to help with their kids. So, as the children's minister said, "We're *desperate* for more volunteers…."

Why do you think that sexual offenders try to infiltrate churches? Because many know that most churches don't even bother checking criminal records. They're too busy. They're small enough that they feel they know everyone. They don't think that convicted sexual offenders will come to *their* church. Why bother checking criminal records when the person is a nice, respectable guy?

The question then comes: How do we protect our church kids from the Mr. Raineses of the world? If child molesters are out there (and they are), we need a plan to build a sufficient firewall around our churches. In the pages ahead, we'll help your church come up with that game plan. But before we describe a plan, our next step is to consider our stewardship of the children in our care.

CHAPTER 2

. . . .

THE STEWARDSHIP OF CHILDREN

One of my favorite times is when I arrive home at the end of a busy workday. Soon after the door shuts, I hear the delighted scream of my three-year-old daughter Eden. "Daaaaadddddyyyyy!" Wherever she is in the house, she comes running to the door. She wraps her tiny arms around my legs and admiringly stares up at me with those adorable brown eyes. Two words come to mind as I look down at her: *absolutely priceless.*

Lest you be mistaken, this is more than just warm fuzzies welling up in my heart. It is a great honor to be Eden's dad. Parenting is a high calling. It's an opportunity to shepherd a soul through life's struggles; to protect her (or him) from all kinds of evil that lurk in this fallen world; and to shape how a child thinks, loves, fears, dreams, and hopes.

What do you think of this calling? Maybe, as a parent, you're just barely getting through the day-to-day battles of diapers, homework, temper tantrums, teenage hormones, and all the other daily trials that come with parenting. You may have lost that twinkle in your eye that you had as a brand new parent, no longer marveling at this child. You are perhaps fighting just to keep your child fed and out of trouble. In which case, you almost certainly need some encouragement and a reminder about what a privilege it is to *be* a parent. Or maybe you are a children's ministry director, a pastor, a

Sunday school teacher, or volunteer in the nursery, and the weekly grind of caring for other people's children is wearing you down. Before we come to understand the dangers that child abusers pose to our children, we must remember our high calling as parents, pastors, and children's ministry workers—the God-given charge to love, protect, and shepherd children under our care.

Why We Have Children

In the beginning, God made Adam and Eve. In recounting this event, Moses wrote,

> Then God said, "Let us make mankind in our image, in our likeness, so that they may rule over the fish in the sea and the birds in the sky, over the livestock and all the wild animals, and over all the creatures that move along the ground."
>
> So God created mankind in his own image, in the image of God he created them; male and female he created them.
>
> God blessed them and said to them, "Be fruitful and increase in number; fill the earth and subdue it. Rule over the fish in the sea and the birds in the sky and over every living creature that moves on the ground" (Genesis 1:26–28).

God created man and woman in his image, which means they were made to reflect his likeness. They were not going to *look like him,* for God is spirit (John 4:24) and doesn't have physical attributes like a nose, eyes, or feet. But they were going to grow to be *like him* in his moral attributes—love, peace, patience, kindness, goodness, etc.

God gives image-bearers the unique responsibility to be his representatives in the garden and to help him steward or "rule" his creation (vv. 26, 28). If God is the great Creator and owner of the garden, Adam and Eve were to be his chief gardeners, zookeepers, and caretakers.

God charges the man and the woman not only with stewarding the garden and caring for the animals but also with having children: "Be fruitful and increase in number; fill the earth and subdue it" (v. 28).

Why does God entrust men and women with this responsibility to multiply? Let me suggest two reasons. First, as men and women reproduce, they fill the earth with image-bearers who will help watch over God's creation. As the children grow up to be gardeners and zookeepers, they will help their parents steward God's wonderful creation. Second, when married couples have children, the earth is filled with more worshippers who, in bearing God's image, reflect his glory back to him.

The Privilege of Stewardship

Parents, pastors, and children's ministry workers all have responsibility to steward the children entrusted to us. What is a steward? It is one who is responsible for watching over someone else's stuff. In this case, God has given our children to my wife and me as a gift (James 1:17), and for as long as we live, we are accountable to him for how we shepherd them through this life (1 Timothy 3:4–5). It is a *privilege* to be given this responsibility. This is very different than caring for a dog or a cat; we are more than just a zookeeper and gardener watching over God's pets and mowing his lawn for him. Our children are worshippers who have an eternal destiny—either heaven or hell. God can use us as parents to help point them to Jesus. What an *enormous* privilege, but what a *weighty* responsibility that is.

Churches also have a responsibility to steward the gift of children. Several hours a week, parents entrust this very precious gift of children to churches—to watch over, instruct, and protect the kids under their care. Church workers should consider the time spent with other people's children not as a burden, but as a great privilege and important responsibility.

As with everything else in the Christian life, parents and church workers can learn from Christ's example, as Jesus shows us how he loves children: "People were bringing little children to Jesus for him to place His hands on them, but the disciples rebuked them. When Jesus saw this, he was indignant. He said to them, 'Let the little children come to me, and do not hinder them, for the kingdom of God belongs to such as these. Truly, I tell you, anyone who will not receive the kingdom of God like a little child will never enter it.' And he took the children in his arms, placed his hands on them and blessed them" (Mark 10:13–16).

While the disciples tried to keep the children and their parents away from Jesus, our Lord welcomed them. The culture in first-century Jerusalem didn't value children. Yet Jesus saw children as having immense importance and value. Jesus presented little children as examples of how to enter the kingdom (v. 15). He stated elsewhere that whoever welcomes children in his name shows that they also welcome Christ and God the Father (Mark 9:36–37). Many Christians today assume they value children, but in practice often treat their children like the disciples did. Consider for yourself: Are you welcoming and valuing children like Jesus did?

Solomon also wrote about little children: "Behold, children are a heritage from the LORD, the fruit of the womb a reward. Like arrows in the hand of a warrior are the children of one's youth. Blessed is the man who fills his quiver with them! He shall not be put to shame when he speaks with his enemies in the gate" (Psalm 127:3–5 ESV). Children are a heritage and a reward. They are *gifts* from God. To have many children—"a quiver full of them"—is to count oneself blessed by God.

Children are also described as arrows. Arrows are useful only when they sit in the hands of a skilled archer. The word picture is one of the blessings of protection for parents. In Solomon's day, there was no such thing as a local police station, so when the Philistines came to raid your farm, parents found security and assistance in having many children. The enemy would take pause when four well-built young men stood on the edge of the property line with swords and scabbards in hand.

So also sons are more useful to a father when they are born "in one's youth" (v. 4). Those who waited to have kids until they were very old would not have children around to protect, assist, or speak up for them when their enemies tried to shame them at the gate (v. 5). The reference to a gate is not what you might think it is—e.g., an entrance to a white picket fence around your house. A gate in Solomon's day was the place where court was held and disputes settled in the community. Children would be a blessing to ailing and elderly parents. In Solomon's day, Social Security and Medicare came in the form of children who would take care of you when you were old.

An important message that emerges from these three texts (Mark 9:34–37; 10:13–16; Psalm 127) is that children are to be cherished, respected, and loved. The great sacrifices that parents and church workers make for kids are not just because they love these kids (which they do!) but more so because they love the great God who has entrusted these kids to them.

The Responsibility to Teach and Protect

Along with the privilege of stewarding the gift of children, parents and church workers do have a fundamental responsibility to point children to the truth. While only God can save children, God uses parents who raise their children "in the training and instruction of the Lord" (Ephesians 6:4) as a means to pass truth on to the next generation. Moses instructed the Israelites,

> Hear, O Israel: The LORD our God, the LORD is one. Love the LORD your God with all your heart and with all your soul and with all your strength. These commandments that I give you today are to be on your hearts. *Impress them on your children.* Talk about them when you sit at home and when you walk along the road, when you lie down and when you get up. Tie them as symbols on your hands and bind them on your foreheads. Write

them on the doorframes of your houses and on your gates. (Deuteronomy 6:4–9, emphasis added)

Later, in Deuteronomy 31:13, Moses says that Israel was to do these things so that "their children, who do not know this law, must hear it and learn to fear the LORD your God." We don't teach the Scriptures to our children so that we can fill their little heads up with lots of Bible facts. Parents, pastors, and children's ministry workers are commanded to communicate the truths of God to children so that these kids will one day fear the Lord.

In addition to teaching their children, Christians also have a fundamental responsibility to protect them. We learn this sense of protection from God, who throughout the Bible has a special burden for the young, weak, and oppressed in society.

He defends the cause of the fatherless and the widow, and loves the foreigner residing among you, giving them food and clothing. (Deuteronomy 10:18)

Learn to do right; seek justice. Defend the oppressed. Take up the cause of the fatherless; plead the case of the widow. (Isaiah 1:17; cf. Jeremiah 7:5–7)

Religion that God our Father accepts as pure and faultless is this: to look after orphans and widows in their distress and to keep oneself from being polluted by the world. (James 1:27)

Children are among the most vulnerable in our society today. God asks us as Christians to help him look after them.

The Hazards of Being Careless or Overprotective

Protecting our children is a high calling given by God himself. To take this calling seriously, we must do more than just protect: we should love, cherish, and guide our children throughout their lives. This work should not be defensive or lackadaisical. At its best it will be proactive, loving, careful, and deliberate. Laziness and carelessness in shepherding of children opens the door for sexual perpetrators to take full advantage of our kids. Sexual offenders are on a quest for pleasure and don't care about the destruction of lives they cause along the way.

Several years ago I was volunteering as the head coach for my four-year-old son's soccer league. Every Saturday morning, I guided fifty or so parents and their children through an hour of exercise, soccer skills, and fun. Most weeks, one particular mom would drop her son off and then leave to spend time at a Starbucks down the road. Almost every time she left him and walked off the field, I thought, "Seriously, you are going to leave such a young child *unsupervised* with all of these strangers?"

Careless and lazy parents are not the only ones who need to be warned. Being a good but naive parent or children's ministry worker can also easily lead to disaster. A normally diligent person drops his guard for a moment and—bam! That could be the very moment of opportunity a sexual predator was waiting for. There are no "re-dos" when it comes to sexual abuse.

Keep in mind, though, that no adult can *perfectly* protect kids from evil in this fallen world. Even homeschoolers, who spend the majority of their time at home or at church, can't avoid the long tentacles of the Internet and social media that reach beyond the walls of our homes and into our children's lives. The sad reality is that no matter how careful we are, some of our children will be abused— and it will likely happen right under our noses. We'll be fooled and we'll hate the fact that we were not "with it" enough to catch the perpetrator before he (or she) did harm. A realistic perspective on life in a fallen world is not that we can perfectly protect our kids but that with wisdom, carefulness, and planning we can reduce the risk. That's our goal from here to the end of the book—to help you think about how to reduce the risk of child abuse in your church.

CHAPTER 3

· · · ·

THE FALSE ASSUMPTIONS WE MAKE

"Assumptions are a deathbed for all who give in to them." That's the line I heard a few days ago from an elderly woman who was recounting her tendency to ruin relationships with unfounded assumptions. Her words probably ring true for you, just as they did for me. You make assumptions every day, don't you? You think of some things as possible, but you have no definitive proof to show if your assumptions are true or not. You *think* they're true, but you can't actually prove them.

Think about the way you fight with your spouse or friends. What often leads you astray are the assumptions you make about the other person. Betty thinks that John doesn't like her because of the way he acts around her. John is really only shy, but Betty worries and does her best to impress him whenever he is around. Betty's thoughts and behaviors toward John are controlled by her assumptions. She is reacting more to the person in her mind (and what she assumes about him) than to the actual person standing in front of her (and what he really thinks).

Every human being is an interpreter. We think, analyze, and make interpretations about the world we live in. We see a certain set of facts, and we use our hearts and minds to analyze what we are seeing. In a fallen world, however, our interpretations will often go astray because we are sinners with corrupt hearts and minds (Romans 3:23), and we are plagued by blind spots (Matthew 7:3).

Sexual offenders get away with what they do because too many people make assumptions about offenders based on stereotypes and limited knowledge. To fight back against this problem, we need to think through four unhelpful assumptions Christians make that can potentially lead us astray.

1. It Will Never Happen to Us

Julie was a loving mother, who doted over her two children. She was very involved in church. She had a good marriage and a caring husband. She was very active in her local community. As a young girl, she had dreamed about one day being a wife and mother. When God gave her a wonderful husband and two adorable children, it seemed life couldn't get much better. It wasn't perfect and it certainly wasn't paradise, but her marriage and children brought an immense amount of joy to her life.

Shortly after Julie's daughter celebrated her seventh birthday, she was molested by the babysitter's boyfriend. The incident happened several times. Soon after the first incident her daughter started to apologize out of the blue, for nothing in particular.

"I'm sorry, Mommy and Daddy."

"Sorry for what, honey?"

Her daughter would often wince at that moment, but not say anything more. Both parents had a hard time getting her to say anything else. After a few instances over the next few days, the spontaneous apologizing stopped.

A few months later, Julie got a phone call from the babysitter's mother. Her daughter (their regular babysitter) had walked in on her boyfriend doing inappropriate things to Julie's daughter. The babysitter had been scared to say anything because her boyfriend had made threats to hurt her, but she had finally confessed what she knew to her mother.

Julie and her husband were crushed. They never imagined this could happen to them. They had seen accounts on the news about abused children, but they never dreamed it would happen to their daughter. The guilt, pain, tears, and anger were almost too much to bear.

We tend to assume these things will never happen to us, even though we know it does happen to someone. We assume our kids are safe—and they generally are. But even if we raised them in protective bubbles, we couldn't completely keep them away from the world, nor could we keep the world away from them.

One year when I was teaching Sunday school to fourth graders, a father named John told me he would deliberately pass over the difficult parts of the Bible (i.e., David's affair with Bathsheba, the rape of Tamar, etc.) when reading to his kids. Sadly, as a result, his kids ended up learning more about sex through their friends and schoolyard banter than they would at home. Another parent, Debbie, limited the kind of movies her kids watched and music they listened to. Yet her kids still found lots of unsavory things on the Internet when she wasn't around.

John and Debbie probably had a false sense of protection for their kids, one that in reality cannot exist. Evil is a real part of the world we live in, and no parents can completely keep their kids away from this corrupt world. Evil is not just something we see in the movies or hear about on the news. It lurks around our kids every day, like a prowling lion (1 Peter 5:8).

Take a moment, and go to one of these free websites that lists the sexual offenders in your community:

National Alert Registry:
    www.nationalalertregistry.com
The Department of Justice Sexual Offender Registry:
    www.nsopw.gov/Core/Portal.aspx

Now, put in your address and see how many sexual offenders live in your town or local community. Surprised? There are probably more than you expected. In my zip code, there were at least eighteen registered sexual offenders. Remember, these are only the ones who have taken the time to register. I'm fairly certain that some don't keep their contact information updated. Some probably do not want the stigma of being known as a sex offender, so there are probably more criminal offenders out there than are listed on these websites. Counseling professor Justin Smith comments, "[since] 1994 [to 2011], there have been 685,515 individuals who have been registered as sex offenders in America. Despite how disturbing these figures are, they do not unmask the true extent of sexual abuse."[1]

We don't want the assumption that it will never happen to us to make us less vigilant in protecting our kids. If we are lured into thinking this way, we won't take all of the necessary steps to protect our children.

2. Sexual Perpetrators Are Monsters, and Not Anything Like Us

If we're honest, we have a profile in our minds when we think about sexual perpetrators. They are almost certainly economically poor. Maybe they have psychiatric problems. They probably have been abused by family or neighbors. They perhaps look unkempt and disheveled. They are the most disrespected and disliked people in our community. Clinical psychologist Carla van Dam describes the stereotypical assumptions people tend to make about sexual offenders:

> A molester was assumed to be a single man who was easily identified by his "seedy" looks and unshaven appearance. He would lurk in the shadows and grab children. He was called the "bogeyman" by some and a "pervert" by all. Other commonly held misconceived ideas were that the sexual offender was visibly insane, mentally retarded, brutal, depraved, immoral, or

oversexed. He was assumed to be a fiend and to spend his time reading or viewing pornography, and he was either an alcoholic or a drug addict. Such popular misconceptions contributed to the belief that the sex offender was somehow not an ordinary person, was easily distinguishable, and was always a male.[2]

Does any of this characterize how you think of sexual offenders? We assume they are not anything like us. We think they're monsters—big, evil, mean creatures who will come out of the shadows to do harm to our kids.

We'll come to see that most of our stereotypes about sexual offenders are not true. In fact, they are a lot more like us than we could have ever imagined. If we sculpt the wrong profile, it will lead us astray from the outset. When we are looking for the wrong enemy, our opponent sneaks past our protective walls. Knowing who the sexual offenders are and what demographics they typically fit will help us to keep a better lookout. We will think much more about the profile of child abusers in Chapter 4.

3. We Know the People in Our Church

After a workshop on child abusers, Judy shared with me that her church didn't do any type of screening for children's ministry workers. She commented, "We ask anyone who is attending to consider helping, but we don't do anything to verify they are safe to work with the kids. We're a small church, so we feel like we know everyone."

Judy's church is not unusual. Just like many other churches, Judy's pastor and fellow church members have given in to the third deadly assumption, that we know the people in our church. When a church believes this, they become less inclined to do any type of screening, and that's what makes a sexual offender's work so easy.

Many churches feel like they know their members well enough to let them work with the kids. Why bother checking? It costs money every time you run a professional screening, and church budgets are often tight, especially in small churches. Many serial child abusers know that churches make these kinds of assumptions. They take advantage of the fact that we are putting our kids at risk.

You've probably heard the news stories where a close friend, coworker, uncle, or neighbor says something like, "I've known him for ten years . . . or at least I thought I knew him. I would never have guessed he would have done something like this." They thought they knew their friend, but in fact they did not.

What's my point? I'm not trying to create a false fear of all people. The Bible tells Christians not to live with a spirit of timidity or fear but one of true hope in the living God. Yet we also know that wherever Christians or religious people are gathered, there are likely to be hypocrites among us. Hypocrites put on external appearances, such that we think we know who they are, but their hearts are full of all kinds of evil. In describing the insincerity of his own chosen people Israel, the Lord God said,

> Their tongue is a deadly arrow; it speaks deceitfully. With their mouths they all speak cordially to their neighbors, but in their hearts they set traps for them. (Jeremiah 9:8)

> These people come near to me with their mouth and honor me with their lips, but their hearts are far from me. (Isaiah 29:13)

Just as there were hypocrites among the people of Israel, so there are hypocrites in our churches.

The Bible tells us to expect hypocrites to be living among us. Jesus stared directly in the face of the most esteemed religious leaders of his day, the Pharisees, and said,

> Woe to you, teachers of the law and Pharisees, you hypocrites! You are like whitewashed tombs, which look beautiful on the outside but on the inside are full of the bones of the dead and everything unclean. In the same way, on the outside you appear

to people as righteous but on the inside you are full of hypocrisy and wickedness (Matthew 23:27–28).

Jesus also chose a man named Judas to be one of his disciples. Judas would become the most famous hypocrite of all time, betraying Jesus to his enemies. Jesus is unique because he can see beyond external appearances and straight down into our hearts. He knows us better than we know ourselves (John 13: 2, 21–30). While we do not have Jesus's ability to see the heart, we do need to be wise and look beyond the surface of people, recognizing that appearances can be deceiving.

4. Our Church Is Safe for Our Kids

Several years ago, I was visiting a church and overheard a parent ask the children's minister, "What type of screening do you do of your children's ministry workers?"

"We don't do anything," she said.

She was surprised, as was I. As a parent she assumed that the church was doing more. Regrettably, she had given herself over to the fourth deadly assumption—her church was safe for her kids. Her church was not disorganized; in fact, it was organized quite well. Her church was not spiritually dead; it was a vibrant and growing congregation. Her church didn't have a small children's ministry department; it was overflowing with parents and kids. Because of the general "health" of her church, this mother assumed they were doing much more to protect the kids from child abusers.

Have you ever asked your children's minister what he or she is doing to protect the kids? Get him to list it for you. Some of you will be thrilled at what has been implemented for the safety and protection of the church's children. Others . . . well, you'll be shocked just like me.

One response might be, "We don't do anything. We're desperate for volunteers and already have a hard time getting people to serve in children's ministry. We don't want to do anything (e.g., trainings, screenings) that will get in the way of people serving quickly." What do you do then? Don't leave the church, especially if there are a lot of good reasons to stay. Help the pastor and children's minster think through the importance of these issues. If they don't do anything to protect the kids, and they *don't care* about doing anything, only then should you consider leaving.

Another response might be, "We do some things, but know we need to do a lot more." Telling your children's minister to just "get on the ball" and get it done won't help much. If she is like the typical children's ministry worker, she is overwhelmed, stressed-out, and short-staffed. Especially if you have kids at stake, it behooves *you* to come alongside the children's minister to help her get this done.

Don't take for granted what your church is doing. The best way to deal with your assumptions is to take time to ask someone who is "in the know" at your church. The safety of the church's children is at stake, and you don't want to gamble with a priceless commodity.

Are You Giving In?

If it is true that assumptions are a deathbed for all who give in to them, then ask yourself: "Have I given in to any of these four deadly assumptions?" As a pastor, children's ministry worker, volunteer, or parent, it is good to know what false assumptions we are making about our children's safety and how to deconstruct them.

Sexual offenders will take advantage of our assumptions. We don't want to give them any room to do harm. If you've made any of these assumptions, don't fear. We've got help ready for you in the chapters ahead as we think about who the child abusers are, how they work, and how we can protect against them.

CHAPTER 4

· · · ·

TYPES, TECHNIQUES, AND TARGETS OF SEXUAL PREDATORS

In November of 2011, all of the major news networks broke stories about former Penn State defensive coordinator Jerry Sandusky, who was accused of sexually abusing at least eight boys over a span of fifteen years. Rather quickly, a dark cloud grew over Penn State. Two administrators left over accusations of a cover-up; the board of trustees fired the president of the school, Graham Spanier, as well as legendary football coach Joe Paterno, who was Sandusky's boss.

In 1977, Sandusky started a foster home for troubled boys, which later turned into a statewide charity. Over the course of several years, Sandusky had enough suspicious and potentially inappropriate encounters with young boys to warrant investigation. A lengthy grand jury investigation in 2010 and 2011 led to the arrest—and a black mark on one of college football's most revered programs. In June of 2012, Sandusky was found guilty and given a thirty-year prison sentence.

Sandusky's life lines up with one of the typical profiles of a sexual predator. He's *not* disheveled and disliked. He *is* someone who is respected and highly revered in his community. He's *not* someone who is poor and socially isolated. He *is* someone who has influence and money. He is *not* someone who abducted a child and forced him to do lewd things. He *is* someone who regularly spent time with troubled children and lavished gifts and special treatment on them. He is *not* someone suspected of being abusive to young children. He *is* someone who was thought to be doing great good for kids through his charity work and adoption of six children.

Are you surprised? Most folks would not have pegged Sandusky as a potential child abuser. But then again most of us make false assumptions about who sexual offenders are and who they are not. How do sexual predators operate? Who do they target? How do they get away with what they do? Those are some of the questions we want to cover in this chapter as we think about the types, techniques, and targets of sexual predators.

The Types of Sexual Predators

There are two types of sexual predators—the *power* predator and the *persuasion* predator.[1] Both wreak great havoc in the lives of their victims. Both are problematic for police, parents, and the societies in which they live, and they have very different ways of accomplishing their evil ends.

The *power predator* takes a child by sheer force. He overtakes his victim by overpowering her and forcing her into captivity. You can think in terms of a child grabbed in a park or a schoolyard, dragged into a car, and driven off without the strength or ability to stop the sexual offender.

Bestselling author and risk-assessment expert Gavin de Beker describes it this way: "The power predator charges like a bear, unmistakably committing to his attack. Because of this, he cannot easily retreat and say there was merely a misunderstanding. Accordingly, he strikes only when he feels certain he'll prevail."[2]

Almost twenty years ago, Jaycee Dugard was a young girl on her way to the school bus when Philip Craig and his wife Nancy Garrido abducted her. Nancy had scouted out Jaycee's path to school, and then one morning, just as Jaycee started walking down the road, the couple drove alongside her. Philip pulled out a stun gun, shocked the girl, and then Nancy pulled her into the back of the car. Philip would later say to his wife, "I can't believe we got away with this."[3] For many years after her abduction, Jaycee was a sex slave, locked up in a shed in the backyard of Philip and Nancy's home. In just one fleeting moment, Jaycee was robbed of her life and childhood innocence. Enduring several years of rape is a nightmare scenario, but Jaycee stayed alive and eventually escaped.[4] Unlike Jaycee, many victims of a power predator are never heard from again.

The *persuasion predator* uses his personality, charm, and influence to convince others that he is trustworthy and then at the right time strikes to abuse children. You might think about the illustration of a wolf in sheep's clothing: The wolf intends to harm others but doesn't want them to discover his plans and so puts on the appearance of an innocent sheep.

In church settings we are often less focused on power predators. If you have a good structural setup in your children's ministry wing (check-in desk, half-doors on classrooms, hall monitors, etc.) and some type of security check-in system, that does a lot to keep the power predator at bay. The persuasion predator is far more likely to infiltrate your church setting.

The Myth of Stranger Danger

One of the most common myths about sexual offenders is that they will be strangers who take away your child. Power predators do exist. They scope out playgrounds or other places with kids to abduct children and steal their lives. Jaycee Dugard knows this reality all too well.

But in church and family settings, our problem is much less often with a stranger than it is with those whose lives regularly intersect with ours: fellow church attenders, childcare workers in the nursery, family members, and neighbors—the people we know, not the people we don't know. Boz Tchividjian, executive director of Godly Response to Abuse in the Christian Environment (G.R.A.C.E.), makes this point: "It is common knowledge that most children are not sexually victimized by strangers. In fact, one study found that only 10 percent of child molesters molest children that they don't know."[5]

Many children are taught from an early age not to talk to strangers. But strangers are not as much of a problem as some who live among us every day. Teaching our children to be wary of strangers can give us a false sense of security. What parents often ignore is the familiar adult who is too friendly with our kids. Consider the following:

- More than eighty percent of the time, victims of child abuse know their abusers.
- Most abuse takes place within the context of an ongoing relationship.
- Some child abusers are married and abuse their own children.[6]

Most children know how to respond to an unwelcome stranger, but they're uncertain what to do when a "safe" adult makes them uncomfortable. Consequently, we will spend much of our time considering how to protect against the "safe" adult who is a persuasion predator.

What Is the Typical Profile for a Sexual Predator?

Pretend you're taking a multiple choice test. Take a look at the list below and make your best guess at who you think might fit the profile for a sexual offender.

A. A young, single male architect
B. A "soccer mom" with four children
C. A pediatrician
D. A Catholic priest
E. A public school teacher
F. None of the above
G. A and D only
H. All of the above

The correct answer is "H." While single males are the most likely, we can't assume this to be the *only* type of predator. There are some instances when women get trapped in this perverse sin. Most commonly, one would think of a school teacher who is leading teenage boys astray with inappropriate sexual encounters. But there are other categories of female offenders, including some with sadistic tendencies, and those who are coerced by a male partner to abuse children.[7]

In fact, predators come in all types—single and married; blue and white collar; educated and uneducated; rich, middle class, and poor. In examining a range of sexual offender cases, I've found examples in almost every category of work—college professor, athletic director of a private school, Catholic priest, doctor, lawyer, pastor, and many other professionals. We can't limit sexual offenders to just one generic profile.

The Techniques of a Sexual Predator

Questions abound when it comes to understanding sexual offenders. How do predators get away with the things that they do? How do they fool the church community and then the child? What methods do they employ to keep children from disclosing their grotesque behavior?

Grooming the Church Community

The most common technique for sexual offenders to gain access to children is to cultivate a double life. Sexual offenders work very hard to be likable and respectable members of a church. If they are liked and respected, they earn the trust of the church community. Once they are trusted, they gain access to children. This is known as "grooming"—a process of working over the children and adults in a church in order to earn their trust.

Offenders don't usually rush through grooming but instead take their time to develop relationships with the members of a church community. In order to win over the adults and become an accepted part of the church, they put on a persona of being useful, kind, helpful, polite, and caring to adults and children alike. Author and expert Anna Salter comments,

> The double life is a powerful tactic: There is the pattern of socially responsible behavior in public that causes parents and others to drop their guard, to allow access to children, and to turn a deaf ear to disclosures. But a surly and obnoxious person would have little access, no matter how proper and appropriate his public behavior was. The second tactic—the ability to charm, to be likeable, to radiate sincerity and truthfulness—is crucial to gaining access to children.[8]

Most violent offenders know enough to keep their behavior in check publicly or else their plans would be ruined. The fact that a sexual offender is not off-putting but might actually have lots of good qualities makes it very difficult to pinpoint one. Most people think of a sexual offender as *all bad* and can't conceive of such a person having anything good about him or her.

Once the sexual predator has gained the trust of a significant number of people within a church, suspicions become harder to articulate. Conformity studies show that few people will publicly disagree with a majority opinion. And if the person gets enthusiastic support from church friends or church leaders, it makes it all the more difficult to speak out against them with persuasive conviction.

In reality, what is happening is that the sexual offender is regularly manipulating and pretending to be someone he or she is not. Offenders are professional liars—very skillful at what they do because they've done it for years. They've lied to everyone in their lives—church members, friends, their victims, and even to themselves—in order to justify their sinful desires and continue on the destructive path of harming children. According to most experts who work with sexual offenders, not only is their lying hard to detect, but it is often quite convincing. [9]

If a predator is roaming around your church, he is probably not a stranger to you. More than likely, he is someone whom you already know, like, and do not see as a threat to your children.

Grooming the Child

Once a predator has earned the trust of a church community and perhaps a particular family, gaining access to children in the process, he will start grooming a child. He will give gifts, words of praise, an extraordinary amount of attention, and show affection to the unsuspecting child. One sexual offender described his strategy this way:

> When a person like myself wants to obtain access to a child, you don't just go up and get the child and sexually molest the child. There's a process of obtaining the child's friendship and, in my case, also obtaining the family's friendship and their trust. When you get their trust, that's when the child becomes vulnerable, and you can molest the child. . . .[10]

Before his arrest and conviction, Jerry Sandusky would take children to football games, special trips, and sleepovers at his home. In a church setting, you might watch out for a teacher or children's ministry worker who repeatedly brings special gifts for one child, who overtly bonds with one particular kid, or who works to gain access to that same child outside of the church.

In regard to physical contact, the grooming of a child occurs across a continuum, starting with more innocent behaviors like touching an arm or tickling games and then gradually moves on to more risky behavior like kissing on the lips instead of the cheek, telling sexual jokes, or extended touch. The sexual predator's goal is to blur the lines between appropriate and inappropriate behavior, which opens the doorway to taking greater risks. Things progress with the child becoming more comfortable with each step, as an increasing level of sexuality is introduced into the relationship.[11]

For example, "Mr. Clay" would ask kids to stay after Sunday school to help out or finish their work. Many parents let their kids remain because Mr. Clay was such a well-respected man in their church community. Those who remained behind got special attention from Mr. Clay. He would start with a simple caress on the back, at first over the shirt. If that was not met with any resistance or was not reported to parents, he would gradually progress to touching underneath the shirt. If children reported this or parents asked about it, he would simply say he was checking for chicken pox and no longer engage the child. But if there was no resistance from the child or reporting to the parents, the physical contact would go further, eventually to genital contact.[12]

In the grooming process, predators spend an unusual amount of time with kids. They engage children in behavior and play that is appropriate for the child's age and prefer to spend more time with children than adults. This should lead observing adults to wonder why this person (an adult or even a teenager) would rather be hanging out more with young kids than their own peers.

Many sexual offenders are very deliberate and careful in their planning. According to prosecutor and expert Victor Vieth, "Sex offenders often look for the easiest target."[13] A prime example is a sexual predator who purposefully pursues more vulnerable children, such as kids with single or divorced parents. Think about what's happening in these families—the child often longs for a father figure, so he or she quickly gravitates toward any type of paternal influence. The single mother is exhausted and desperately needs help, so she all too quickly gives over the care of her kids to an interested adult in order to get a break.

What other types of vulnerable children might sexual predators be targeting? Offenders will prey on children who are experiencing family problems; children who are often in trouble; kids who are eager to please; kids who are picked on by other children; kids who are quiet, withdrawn, and isolated; kids who are disabled in some way that might make them less believable (e.g., cognitively disabled children); or kids who are too young to articulate the experience of abuse. Note what sex offender John Henry said in his testimony before the US Senate:

> I showed them affection and the attention they thought they were not getting anywhere else. *Almost without exception, every child I have molested was lonely and longing for attention.* . . . Their desire to be loved, their trust of adults, their normal sexual playfulness and their inquisitive minds made them perfect victims (emphasis added).[14]

One important lesson for Christian parents is that children who are not craving an adult's attention are less likely to be targeted by a predator. Parents, take heed and love your children. Love them so that they won't feel the need to seek the attention of another adult in order to get the love they should be getting from you. Consistent parental love can make a difference and can help your children to be less vulnerable to predators.

Counting on No Disclosure

Children who are molested and disclose this to an adult are rarely taken seriously because their perpetrators seem unlikely to be sexual offenders. If your child said his school teacher, doctor, or soccer coach molested him, would you immediately believe him? Most of us want to say, "Yes, of course we would." Yet, in reality, many parents would struggle with discerning between the folly of a child (Proverbs 22:15) and the reputation of a highly respected, well-known figure in the community.

Attorney General Linda Kelly commented after Jerry Sandusky's trial, "One of the recurring themes of the witnesses' testimony, which came from the voices of the victims themselves in this case, was, 'Who would believe a kid?'"[15]

Only a small minority of children will disclose abuse at the time it is occurring. Not surprisingly, sexual predators who are concerned about children disclosing (some are, some are not) will try to convince the child to keep it a secret. The following is taken from a "Q-and-A session" with a sexual offender:

Question: How do you keep your victims from telling?

Answer: Well, first of all I've won all their trust. They think I'm the greatest thing that ever lived. Their families think I'm the greatest thing that ever lived. Because I'm so nice to them and I'm so kind and so—there's just nobody better to that person than me. If it came down to, you know…. "I have a little secret, this is our little secret," then it would come down to that, but it doesn't have to usually come down to that. It's almost an unspoken understanding.[16]

Sadly, children are too often ignored, which in turn increases the sexual offender's confidence level and his willingness to take risks. A dreadful consequence of children keeping secrets or not being believed by adults is that most offenders will end up with dozens of victims before they are ever caught.[17]

Counting on Privacy
Many child abusers count on privacy in order to avoid being caught. If a church works at crafting an environment and policies that don't allow children to be isolated with adults, it becomes more difficult for an offender to abuse a child.[18] That's why an adequate child protection policy will have guidelines such as a two-adult rule, highly visible classrooms, and prohibiting corporal punishment in church.

However, some offenders will abuse even when other adults or children are present. One study showed that fifty-five percent of child molesters will abuse a child with other children present, while twenty-four percent will abuse with another adult present. Abuse in this form is not explicit but many times subtle and hard to detect. Examples include the teacher fondling the child behind the table or a father groping his daughter under the bedsheets while the mother is asleep.[19]

How could someone be so bold as to abuse when others are around? Some offenders take risks, and as their risks are successful and go undetected, their confidence increases, and it feeds a dreadful cycle of more risky attempts. Some offenders are just downright prideful about their ability to fool others. As one offender states:

> There was a great amount of pride. Well, I pulled this one off again. You're a good one. . . . There were times when little old ladies would pat me on the back and say, "You're one of the best young men that I have ever known." I think back and think "If you really knew me, you wouldn't think that."[20]

Other offenders like the thrill of power, being able to dominate someone else, or the fact that they can abuse anywhere, at any time they want, and with anyone present.

The Targets of Sexual Predators

Sexual offenders typically target settings that provide lots of access to children—Boy Scout troops, overnight camps, video game centers or malls, and even churches. Most sexual predators are not looking for a challenge. They want to go someplace where they can have easy access to children.

Some offenders target churches because, in their minds, religious people are easier to fool than most other folks. Christians want to love, serve, forgive, and build trust. We believe that God can change anyone and anything because he has the power to do so. We want to be *hopeful* about our relationships. A sexual offender's aim is to exploit these Christian ideals and turn them into weaknesses. Sometimes, Christians are less inclined to be skeptical about people (or too quick to dismiss our skepticism) because of our redemptive desires for them. A degree of healthy skepticism is necessary to keep sexual predators at bay. In protecting our kids, we want to strike a balance between genuine hope in God and a realistic outlook on the depravity of human beings.

Wolves and Sheep

What would a wolf in sheep's clothing do? He'd walk around pretending to "baaah" like a sheep, making friends with other sheep so that no one would suspect his mischievous plans. Then, at just the right time, he would pounce on one of the most vulnerable sheep.

In order to fight any battle successfully, you must know your enemy. Sexual predators are evil. They deceive and manipulate in order to gain access to children. This chapter has exposed their types, techniques, and targets. Now we will take things one step further, considering the question of why some abusers target churches specifically.

CHAPTER 5

. . . .

WHY THE CHURCH?

Christa was a typical "church girl." She went to church every time the doors were open. She was involved in youth group, had lots of friends, read her Bible, and at the same time was mired in the dilemmas of puberty such as pimples, social cliques, and crushes on the popular boys in school.

Eddie was a typical youth pastor, or so everyone thought. Everyone at First Baptist Church of Farmers Branch liked Eddie a lot. The kids had more fun there than at the other churches in town. And so, unsurprisingly, Eddie's youth group grew fast. The kids found him easy to relate to—obviously a good quality for a youth leader. The church liked him so much they bought him a new station wagon so he could drive around more kids.

Eddie drove kids home after church events. Christa was usually the last one to be dropped off. Things started innocently with small talk on the way home. When they parked in front of Christa's house, they would sit with the lights out and talk for a long time. Topics changed over time. They got more and more personal, and eventually Eddie crossed the line.

"Do you know what obsession means?" Eddie proceeded to explain to Christa how he was obsessed with kissing her. She didn't know what to say. She had never kissed anyone before. "Will you let me kiss you?"

"No." She tried to soften it: "You're like a big brother or uncle to me. I just don't understand."

"Silly goose." That's what he'd call her sometimes. "I can see you're not ready. Go home and pray about it. We'll talk again."

Eddie kept up the pressure, and eventually Christa gave in. And things moved fairly quickly from there. Kissing progressed to groping, to undressing, and eventually to sex—sex in the car, in Eddie's office, even in other people's homes when Christa was babysitting for a family and the kids had gone to sleep.

Christa was often confused. Eddie was married; how could this be right? He would often justify their actions in the eyes of God: "Christa, God has predetermined that we're to be together. It's already written in His plan, and He will make a way for it to happen. Your task is to live by faith and to stop fighting it. His ways aren't our ways, and it's not for us to try to understand." Eddie repeated this regularly, and Christa tried hard to trust him. After all, she wanted to feel special, and she desperately wanted to be a part of God's plan. Eddie told her she had to keep her special role a secret. No one could know.

Who was she to question Eddie? He was an adult, and he worked for the church, after all. "O ye of little faith" is what he would tell Christa whenever she second-guessed him. He would use Jesus's own words to manipulate Christa anytime she resisted.

Eddie was much more than just a youth leader. He was a sexual predator. He continued in his evil ploy to sexually abuse Christa because he got away with it. She told a few people, including the music minister, but none of them helped her. He told her to keep it quiet. Her sister called her a "slut." So she resolved not to say anything and kept it quiet for years. Eddie was able to continue unharmed.

Christa Brown's story is factual.[1] It's not make-believe. The Eddies of this world are out there, and they are abusing and manipulating our children.

Real Christians and Fake Ones

In light of this, two questions are important to consider: First, what is the difference between a real Christian and a fake one? Second, why do these offenders come to churches? In other words, why do these people succeed in doing what they do?

First, we need to remember that sin is rebellion against God (Genesis 3; Romans 6:23). It is choosing to go our own way, to follow our own desires, and turn our back on God. It is a rejection of God as King, and it is an enthronement of oneself, a choice to live life in whatever way we want. We don't care what God thinks or says; we want our own way.

True believers are sinners who have turned from going their own disastrous ways, have been born again (John 3), and trust in Christ as their Lord and Savior (John 1:12; Romans 3:12–26; 5:12–21). Christians know that they need help. Because of their sin, they deserve the punishment of death and eternal separation from God (Romans 3:23). Their sin makes them self-dependent, self-righteous, and self-deceived (2 Corinthians 1:9; Romans 10:3; James 1:16). Finding treasures, pleasure, and satisfaction from the world is a vain pursuit that always leaves a person empty (Ecclesiastes 1:1). Christians know that true and lasting hope can only be found in the Savior, Jesus Christ.

We'll deal with the question of whether a sexual offender can ever become a Christian in Chapter 16. For now, we'll make the case that most child abusers are pretending to be Christians. They are sinners who live for themselves. They are ruled by their selfish desires for sex and power. They lie, cheat, manipulate, and hurt others, leaving a trail of destruction behind them wherever they go. They are in rebellion against God and don't care about the eternal consequences of their sin. They put on a religious persona in order to deceive.

A church is a hospital for sinners who know they need a savior. It is a gathering of Christians who have covenanted together in a local assembly and have committed to following Christ together.

Real Christians and fake ones go to church for very different reasons. True believers are sinners who know they need a savior, but they also need each other to make it through the Christian life. In contrast, sexual offenders are hypocrites who go to church to get easy access to children. They often put on fake religious personas and try to infiltrate churches by pretending to be Christians. They don't go to church for Christian fellowship or to grow in Christ, but to continue their patterns of abuse.

Ultimately, only God can tell the difference between a real and a fake, because only God can see into our hearts (Romans 2:16). Much of the point of this book is to find ways to reduce the risk of hypocrites gaining access to church kids. But, prior to tactical and practical conversations later in the book about how to protect against sexual offenders, we want to make clear the spiritual reality of this situation—most sexual offenders are religious hypocrites; frauds and charlatans; lying to get their own way.

Why Do Sexual Predators Go after Churches?

Sexual offenders do infiltrate churches. But why? What do they see in Christians or churches that make them think this is a good place to abuse children? Let's consider six reasons.

Christians Are Naive

Some sexual offenders state outright that they go to churches because they see Christians as naive. Anna Salter comments, "If children can be silenced and the average person is easy to fool, many offenders report that religious people are even easier to fool than most people."[2]

Christians are, generally speaking, trusting folks. Child abusers recognize this fact and want to take full advantage of it. In the words of one offender,

I consider church people easy to fool. . . . [T]hey have a trust that comes from being Christians. . . . They tend to be better folks all around. And seem to want to trust in the good that exists in people. . . . I think they want to believe in people. And because of that, you can easily convince, with or without convincing words.[3]

If I said that the best disposition for any children's ministry staff or volunteers is to maintain a position of healthy skepticism toward others, many folks would call me a pessimist. And if I took it one step further by asking the church to hold anyone who works with children or youth (even leaders) accountable using screening procedures and child-safety policies, most people would think I've taken this talk about abuse a little too far. It's hard enough to convince many churches to do background checks, let alone establish clear policies and procedures for protecting children. A former prosecutor of sexual offenders has stated, "For a variety of reasons, we naively tend to automatically lower our guard when we are amongst professing Christians. This same naiveté is why offenders flock to the faith community; no other environment provides them such quick and easy access to children without fear of raising concerns."[4]

Christians Are Ignorant of the Problem

Too many Christians are ignorant of the problem of abuse, especially when it happens in churches, and because they don't know the extent of the problem, they don't guard against it. This kind of ignorance leads to a naiveté that can make children vulnerable.

Trial lawyer and sex-abuse expert Kelly Clark gives a good example of how this can happen. He talks about a small Bible church in Oregon that he sued. The school had hired two young men as basketball coaches but didn't run background checks. Several girls were abused by the coaches. Clark explains that the two young men would never have been hired if the checks had been run. He lists several reasons for the school's failure, including this one: "There was a sense that, given the mission that those in leadership at the church had, they felt they were doing the Lord's work. They simply did not believe that such a tragedy could happen, or that God would allow it to happen here. It may be harsh to call this grandiosity, perhaps it was just naiveté, but the result was the same."[5]

Many Christians don't know how to distinguish likeability and trustworthiness. They confuse the two categories, assuming that if someone is courteous and nice, they must also be trustworthy.[6] Moreover, some Christians behave as though the problem doesn't exist, and some look with suspicion on reports of abuse. They believe children are lying and are more prone to take an adult's word. Sexual predators know that these dynamics operate in churches, and they know they can get away with a lot on account of it.

Abuse of Authority

From an early age children are taught to obey authority, especially their parents (Exodus 20:12) or other adults. Authority in the hands of a truly godly person is a good thing and is meant to reflect the character of God. But authority in the hands of an evil person can do great harm to a child.

Child abusers will use positions of spiritual authority to gain access to children and abuse them. Ask yourself: If a pastor or priest walks into the room, what's your normal disposition? Most of us have a degree of caution around strangers until we've gotten to know them and built a trusting relationship. But pastors and priests are often afforded trust just because of their position as clergy.

In one of the most highly publicized cases of abuse among Catholics, Father Lawrence Murphy abused more than two hundred boys in a renowned deaf school in Wisconsin, despite the boys' repeated pleas to priests, nuns, police, and prosecutors for help. From 1950 to 1974, Murphy worked at the school and sexually molested students, at times doing it with other boys in clear sight of his actions. Three successive archbishops were told about Murphy's activities, but not one reported it to the police.

In 1974, Murphy was quietly moved away to northern Wisconsin to live with his mother and continue his work as a priest. For the remaining twenty-four years of his life, he freely worked among children in the parishes and Catholic schools in his area.

In 1993, after repeated complaints about Murphy, Archbishop Rembert Weakland of Wisconsin hired a social worker who specialized in treatment of sexual offenders to interview Murphy about possible allegations of abuse. Probably the most shocking element of this case is that Father Lawrence fully admitted to abusing boys in the deaf school, but for the remaining years of his life he was never prosecuted, either by the church's own court system or by civil authorities. In 1996, Weakland attempted to have Murphy defrocked for his admission, but the Vatican declined to grant a canonical trial to make this possible. Two years later Murphy died and was buried with full priestly vestments. Thus, he not only died without ever facing the earthly consequences for his actions but even in death was treated like any other Catholic priest.[7]

Attitudes of Invincibility or Grandiosity

As in the case of Father Murphy, when religious authority figures abuse children, there is often an attitude that the normal rules of society don't apply to them. Pastors and priests are set apart and anointed by God to teach God's Word and lead God's people. Thus, the clergy grow to think of themselves as unique because of their distinct calling. There can be an attitude of arrogance and grandiosity that causes these abusers to justify their behavior and deny any wrongdoing simply because of their special status. Kelly Clark says that abusers who are clergy are convinced that "their work, their mission, their calling, is so noble, so pure, so divinely inspired, that the laws of human nature or the laws of human society do not apply to them as they do to everyone else."[8]

Manipulation of Religious Roles and/or Language

Child abusers will exploit children in order to accomplish their evil intentions. They will use religious roles or distort religious language as a means to an end—satisfying their own sexual desires by abusing children.[9]

In churches, a religious role gives an abuser a "cover"—a reason to be with children and a way to disguise their evil intentions. Offenders can play the role of a nursery worker, Sunday school teacher, camp supervisor, youth minister, or clergy, and will use their religious cover to gain unfettered access to children, and in turn, to abuse them. Children are expected to show respect to an adult whose job is to demonstrate God's love and teach truth to children. What child would question a nursery worker or Sunday school teacher or pastor or youth minister and suspect him or her of having sinister intentions? Certainly none of mine would.

Along with their religious cover, abusers will also use religious language to confuse a child's understanding of God, sin, or faith. An offender might tell a child that he is loving the child when in fact he is abusing him. The child might have a sense that he is sinning in some way, especially if he hears from his parents or the church that sex outside of marriage is sin. But when a Sunday school teacher or pastor or priest tells him something like, "God told me to do this, so you must obey me," or, "This is not sin, but love," the child will not only be confused but will be inclined not to second-guess a religious authority figure. Add to this the fact that many parents never talk about sex at home. Their kids don't have proper categories for what is happening to them when they are abused, and they are likely to just go along with it.

Accessibility of Children

Because churches are always looking for help with children's ministry and often are facing shortages of volunteers, sexual offenders know that churches are desperate. In children's ministry, volunteers are often late. Some cancel at the last minute when they had promised to volunteer. Others don't even bother showing up for their service. So, when a courteous, kind, reliable man walks in and offers to help, who's going to turn him down?

No other organization provides such quick and easy access to children. Sexual predators know this, so they show up at churches, eager to make themselves known and ready to serve.

Cheap Grace

If a sexual offender is actually caught, he or she counts on what Dietrich Bonhoeffer referred to as cheap grace—grace that comes freely and with very little cost. Abusers are not dumb. They know that if they cry, offer words of contrition, and promise never to do it again, they are very likely not to have to face significant consequences. Pastors and churches are very forgiving. They are quick to apply the gospel—and very, very slow to apply the consequences that come from the law.[10]

The typical offender will say something like, "I'm soooo sorry (tears rolling down his face). This was wrong; and I promise I will never do this again." He is very emotional and, from the look of it, appears to be broken over his sin. What would you do? I'd venture to say too many of us would remind him of God's love for him, let the whole thing go, and put the incident(s) behind us. But sadly, when we do that, we embolden the offender to hurt children again because he got away with it.

Are We Defenseless?

Dreadful situation, isn't it? As you consider the reasons why a child abuser might visit your church, you come to understand why abuse is so common.

We know that the Bible tells us there is evil in this world, and so we should be "wise as serpents and innocent as doves" (Matthew 10:16).

We can't deal with this problem on our own. As Christians we have God on our side. He will help us to be wise.

The million-dollar question is, "What can we do about this?" That's where we turn next as we consider a comprehensive strategy to fight child abuse in churches.

Eight Strategies
for Protecting Against
Abuse

CHAPTER 6

. . . .

CREATING AND IMPLEMENTING
A CHILD PROTECTION POLICY

Look at the following three scenarios, and think about what's wrong with each of them:

Scenario #1: A child of a first-time visitor starts to act out and give the teachers a very hard time. One of the teachers, Mr. Smith, is a kind, older gentlemen, who takes the boy into the hallway, briefly addresses his behavior, and has him sit in a chair for a ten-minute time-out.

Scenario #2: Two childcare workers are watching a group of four- and five-year-olds in the church nursery. One of the girls has to go to the bathroom, so the female volunteer takes her down the hallway to the girl's room, while the male volunteer stays behind, watching the rest of the kids.

Scenario #3: A boy and his mother are given matching bracelets at the children's ministry check-in desk. At the end of the service, she returns and says to the childcare volunteer in the boy's classroom, "Oops. I must have lost my parent identity bracelet. Sorry about that." Feeling the awkwardness of the moment, the volunteer responds with a quick, "No worries. It happens all of the time." The mother takes her son and heads home.

In each of these situations, the volunteers have compromised the care and safety of the children, as I'll explain below. How can you prevent problems like this from occurring in your church?

Creating a Child Protection Policy (CPP)

A child protection policy (CPP) is a set of self-imposed guidelines that describes how a church intends to protect and care for the children under its care. An important part of fighting abuse is planning ahead. You create and implement a CPP because you want to define the parameters for a safe environment for your children *before* a problem arises in your church.

A CPP helps to ensure that your children's ministry leaders, teachers, and other volunteers don't make the mistakes we just read about. Let's see what difference a CPP could make in each scenario.

In Scenario #1 a male teacher isolated himself with the visiting child. A typical CPP will make clear that adults should never be alone with the children. Other adults should always be present when you are watching over the kids. At our church the CPP states in a section on appropriate discipline for children: "Correction should be discrete; in the classroom (not in the hallway); and never outside of the sight of others."[1] This gives the teacher very clear guidelines for where discipline can or cannot occur. Instead of isolating himself with the child, the teacher should have corrected the child in the classroom, rather than out in the hallway by himself. Because child abuse will often happen in isolation, we design policies that prevent a child from being alone with an adult. We lower the risk of abuse when others are present. Moreover, many of the CPP guidelines are protection not only for the kids but also for the adults. If the child in the above scenario later made false accusations against the teacher, saying things about what he said and did, what could the teacher do? He would have no way to protect himself against false accusations because he isolated himself with the child.

In Scenario #2 the volunteers were again breaking the "two-adult rule." To make sure the children are never isolated with just one adult, our CPP states that there must be at least two adults present in the classroom at all times. Churches have different ways of dealing with this. In our church, if a restroom is down the hallway (and not directly attached to the classroom), we have a hall monitor available who is summoned by walkie-talkie and who stays in the classroom until the female volunteer returns with the child from the restroom break. And to make sure the female volunteer is not isolated with the child in the bathroom, she asks a hall monitor to join her. In both the restroom and the classroom, the point is to avoid isolating the adult with a child.

In Scenario #3, the parent was allowed to take the child without showing proper identification. When a wristband or security tag is lost by the parent, a good CPP will have procedures that volunteers will follow to ensure the security of the child. One CPP manual that deals with this situation states, "In the event that a parent loses their security tag, they will be asked to show their driver's license and the desk attendant or service coordinator will match this to the child using the computer system. The children's safety is our first priority, even if it requires extra time."[2] The volunteer in our example let her fear of embarrassment put the child at risk.

As you can see, the purpose of the CPP is to create a safe environment for the children. The main point of children's ministry is not just to teach truth to kids (though this is very important!), or simply to provide adequate care for the children, but to facilitate the parents' ability to participate in the services of the church without having to worry about their children's protection and care. If a church's ministry to the kids is *ad hoc* and not well planned out, the kids and the parents will suffer.

While it might seem self-evident that the main purpose of a CPP is to ensure the safety of the kids (after all, it is a *child protection* policy), the policy's perceived purpose may vary depending on whom you ask. For example, an insurance company's primary goal is to limit liability to the church. That's not the same thing as creating a safe environment for the children, though these goals are not mutually exclusive. So if your insurance company gives you a sample policy, you need to keep their main goal (limiting liability) in mind as you assess the usefulness of the policy. Likewise, as you write your own policy, be clear about what your goal is, and state it upfront in the document.

Functioning without a CPP is a recipe for disaster. A lot of churches, especially smaller ones, do most things informally. Smaller churches have a family-friendly feel—"We're like a family" or "We *all* know each other." The assumption is, "Because we are small, we surely know each other well enough to trust each other." As we saw in Chapter Three, false assumptions like this open the door to predators taking advantage of our children. A good CPP will require screening procedures for everyone who works with children in a formal capacity, no matter how large or small the church.

Decreasing Isolation and Increasing Accountability

Two general principles help to keep kids safe and should typically undergird your CPP. First, *the risk of abuse increases when a child is isolated with an adult.*[3] Many offenders look for privacy in order to commit abuse, so try to ensure that an adult is never isolated with children.

Second, *the risk of abuse increases as accountability decreases.* If an adult is alone with a child, there is no accountability from another adult. Or if a children's event occurs without any knowledge of the leadership or the staff, then there is not accountability from the church as a whole.

Both principles can help your church to assess the level of risk in any particular situation and to implement your policies in a way that makes children's ministry at your church a safe place for kids.[4] Risk-lowering factors will include the following:
- increasing the number of adults present;

- hosting children's ministry activities on church property rather than a private home;
- hosting at a time when more people will be around;
- increasing the visibility of adults and children;
- organizing the setup such that there are clear physical boundaries that "fence in" childcare workers and children and keep out everyone else;
- cultivating a personal knowledge of the character and integrity of the staff or volunteers;
- ensuring that staff and volunteers have participated in the church's training and screening procedures (including a background check and references);
- fostering a high degree of openness about children's ministry classes and events; and
- requiring approval of children's ministry activities by church leadership or staff.

We cannot ever completely eliminate abuse from this world, but we can be deliberate in taking steps that lower the risk of it in our churches. For example, contrast the following situations:

Scenario #1: Two unrelated adult teachers are present in a children's class that occurs at 9:30 a.m. on Sunday morning. The top half of the Dutch door is left open at all times. The class meets in the main building of the church, and there are other classes going on simultaneously in the same hallway.

We would consider this a low-risk situation. Two adults are present, so that the children are not left alone with one adult. The adults are unrelated, since spouses or siblings are often unwilling to report on a relative—or sometimes, even worse, conspire together to harm children. Because the class occurs at 9:30 a.m. on a Sunday morning in the main hallway for children's ministry at the church, there are plenty of other people around, including adults who stop in the class to pick up the attendance sheet or a hall monitor who checks in with the teachers to see if they need anything.

Now, consider Scenario #2: A married couple hosts a game night for youth at their home on a Friday night at 6 p.m. The parents are encouraged to drop off the kids and are told they don't have to stick around. The husband and wife have neither been trained nor screened by staff.

We would consider this a much higher-risk situation. The adults are related to one another. Parents drop off their kids, so no one else is around to hold this married couple accountable. The staff have not checked into the background of this couple, and yet they still give them direct access to kids. The event occurs at a private home rather than the church, which also increases the risk.

In real life, it is inevitable that some situations will be less than ideal, so our goal is to find ways to lower the risk of abuse. For example, at the youth game night, we'd reduce the risk by asking a few parents to stick around, by making sure the staff know about the event, and by asking the couple to go through the church's training and screening before they host a youth game night.

As you think about how to implement your policies, you want to teach the following principle as a part of your training of staff and volunteers: *In order to keep our kids safe, we must always work to decrease isolation and increase accountability.*

The Nuts and Bolts of a CPP

What is typically in a CPP? The context, facilities, and size of the church will create differences in policy, but a basic CPP might include the following:

- The Vision and Mission for Children's Ministry
- Parameters for the Policy
- A Personnel Summary
- General Guidelines and Expectations
  - Expectations for *all* staff and volunteers
  - Training and screening procedures

- ~ Expectations for classrooms, including the two-adult rule, adult-to-child ratios, appropriate and inappropriate discipline, appropriate and inappropriate physical touch, and food and drink guidelines.
- Protective Rules and Safety Guidelines
  - ~ Sickness vs. wellness guidelines
  - ~ Check-in and checkout procedures
  - ~ Restroom procedures
  - ~ Transportation guidelines
  - ~ Off-site or out-of-town event guidelines
  - ~ Emergency response plan and evacuation procedures
  - ~ A plan for preventing, reporting, and responding to child neglect and abuse
  - ~ Guidelines for how the church handles sexual offenders who regularly attend or join the church
  - ~ A duty-to-warn policy
- Appendices:
  - ~ Signs and symptoms of abuse
  - ~ Code of ethics for leadership, staff, or volunteers
  - ~ Sample of the screening application and all children's ministry forms (incident report, medical consent, transportation consent)
  - ~ State guidelines for mandatory or permissive reports

You put guidelines into your CPP only if they have a clear purpose; you don't add rules just for the sake of having rules. A CPP might state something like: "Children under the age of five must be taken to the restroom by a female only." Why is that? Most sexual predators are men, and so we want to have the most vulnerable children taken to the restroom by women, not men. Granted, many of the guidelines have nothing to do with child abusers, like maintaining universal precautions to protect against sickness, limiting food available in the nursery to protect children with allergies, etc.

In writing a CPP, you want to strike a balance between general principles and specific policy statements. Principles trace the values and guidelines that undergird the CPP, while specific policy statements add enough detail so the staff and volunteers know how the principles work in their own specific context. Your CPP is a policy manual, so it will state some principles, but mostly it will be filled with specific policy guidelines.

Be careful of extremes. On the one hand, don't try to write specific guidelines for every conceivable situation. That will make the policy too detailed and will result in the staff getting frustrated because the volunteers don't remember all the details, nor does anyone obey to the full extent of the law. If your policy is not enforceable, it needs to be rewritten so that it can be fully implemented.[5] On the other hand, don't trace out a few general principles and then leave it to each individual volunteer to figure out what to do in specific situations. This too can have disastrous results.[6]

Let's consider an example of a general principle and then consider a specific policy that flows out of it. A general principle that reflects our knowledge of how child abusers work is as follows: *Risk of abuse increases when a child is isolated with an adult.*[7] *Sexual offenders often commit abuse in private settings where there is no accountability.* If we only included this principle in the policy, volunteers would be left to figure out on their own if they've isolated a child or not. We must give staff and volunteers enough direction by also stating clear classroom guidelines like, "For all children's classes and programs, at least two qualified, nonrelated adult volunteers must be present in each classroom at all times," or, "When children's programs or classes are in session, the interior doors and windows should allow for unobstructed views of the room."

A more detailed list of what should be included in a CPP is included in Appendix A of this book, along with a few thoughts on the process of writing (or rewriting) your guidelines. If you don't have a CPP, or don't think your CPP is thorough enough, you can use our suggestions to help write (or rewrite) your own guidelines and procedures.

Implementing a Child Protection Policy (CPP)

A CPP should not be an arbitrary set of rules and guidelines. If no one cares and no one follows it, then the policy is doing you no good. A CPP should actively define how your children's ministry operates. Leaders, Sunday school teachers, and childcare volunteers should generally know what is in it and should be working to follow the guidelines.

Legally, if your church is negligent in providing a reasonable level of care or adhering to its own policies, the church is more vulnerable to lawsuits and carries greater liability. As one court has stated: "As a general rule, a person who undertakes the control and supervision of a child, even without compensation, has the duty to use reasonable care to protect the child from injury. Such a person is not an insurer of the safety of the child. He is required only to use reasonable care commensurate with the reasonably foreseeable risk of harm."[8] Children will get hurt, get into fights with one another, throw things, and do many other foolish things (Proverbs 22:15). Consequently, churches can't guarantee perfect safety, but they can avoid negligence by providing a reasonable level of supervision. Moreover, if your church does nothing formal to protect the children (no CPP, no training or screening of volunteers, etc.) or creates a set of policies and procedures and doesn't abide by them, it has significantly increased the risk of negligence. None of us follows any set of guidelines or rules perfectly in this world. But if the church were to be sued by someone, one of the things the judge would assess is whether or not the church did its best to abide by its own self-imposed policies.[9] As one set of experts state: "Policies create a self-imposed duty of care. As a result, failure to keep policies can help establish the basis of negligent supervision."[10]

How might this play out practically? Pretend a four-year-old child got seriously hurt in a church's preschool classroom and the parents felt like the church was negligent in caring for the child. How could the church show that it attempted to create a safe environment for the child? There are several questions I would want to ask in this situation:

Did the church have developmentally appropriate adult-child ratios for the classroom? A typical CPP will set the ratio of adults-to-children that is "safe" for a particular age group. Our church's CPP states that the ratio for three-to-five-year-olds is one adult for every eight children. If there were only two adults for twenty-five or thirty four-year-olds, the church might already be found negligent based on its own policy.

Did the church have a response plan for medical staff? There should be a procedure in the CPP that helps quickly summon medical staff to the children's ministry wing in case of an emergency. At the very least, there should be a policy related to contacting parents and/or 911 in response to such an emergency.

Did the church have a way to notify parents of an injury? What if the injury didn't seem serious at first but turned into something much worse later on? If this could have been prevented by talking with the parents at checkout and advising follow-up with appropriate medical staff, then the church would not be found negligent.

In the case of child abusers, the same principle applies: Can the church show it did everything it could to protect the children? Did it create policies that guard against child abuse and then implement them?

Take the same four-year-old, and now let's say that she had been abused by a volunteer in the church. In this case I would ask the following:

Did the church have screening procedures? If the volunteer was given immediate access to children in response to his expressed desire to help, the church is likely to be labeled as careless.

Was the sexual offender ever given access to the child alone? A CPP that requires two adults to be present at all times prohibits a sexual offender from being alone with a child.

If a volunteer was suspicious about inappropriate behavior of another volunteer and/or abuse of a child, were there clear guidelines about whom to report to and what to report? The CPP should trace out clear procedures to follow if a volunteer is suspicious and especially if that volunteer is a mandatory reporter.

As we sort out this question of church liability, keep in mind the overall goal of a CPP—to create a *child* protection policy, not a *church* protection policy. But in keeping your focus on this overall goal of protecting children, you'll find that in the end the church is also protected from liability.

Not Convinced Yet?

I'm working hard to persuade you that a CPP is important for your church. Our primary goal in writing and implementing a CPP is to create a safe environment and to protect the kids. But to press you a little further, let's consider seven more reasons why every church should have a CPP:[11]

Your church needs a CPP in order to satisfy your insurance company's requirement for a policy. In order to reduce the risk of abuse and liability, your insurance company will ask you to come up with a policy to protect the children.

Your church needs a CPP in order to satisfy your legal counsel's request for a policy. Not every lawsuit against a church is automatically going to end up in a large award to the victim. If the church's legal counsel can show that the church *did* take child safety seriously as evidenced by a CPP that was consistently implemented by staff and volunteers, it goes a long way in showing that the church at least tried.

A CPP will help define roles and protect staff and volunteers. Clear policies help keep staff and volunteers from making mistakes that put kids at risk and create greater liability. Do you remember the example at the start of the chapter, when the teacher isolated himself with a visiting child in order to correct his bad behavior? That teacher makes himself more vulnerable to false accusations by the child if there are no other adults present. A church who takes this seriously is saying to its staff and volunteers, "You are important to us, and we don't want to put you in jeopardy." A clear CPP helps the staff and volunteers know what to expect and what their responsibilities are toward the children in normal class situations (like a Sunday school class or youth group) and in crisis (like an evacuation during a fire).

A CPP creates an opportunity to talk about abuse. Abuse happens in secret as abusers manipulate children to do unspeakable things. A church that writes and implements child protection guidelines helps the church *as a whole* start a conversation that takes the secret things out of the darkness and brings them into the light (Ephesians 5). By talking about abuse, planning for prevention and response, training volunteers, and starting a conversation, the church makes a clear statement to offenders that it is not going to be passive about this issue.

A CPP will define clear guidelines for reporting and responding to abuse. If abuse does occur, do the volunteers and staff know who to contact and what to say? A reliable policy helps workers know whom to talk to, what the process of reporting abuse should look like, and how to care for the abuse victims.

A CPP creates clear guidelines for how a church should interact with sexual offenders. What if a known sexual offender comes to your church? A CPP should trace how the church will interact with the abuser if he attends regularly or asks to join the church.

A CPP helps preserve our gospel witness. To the extent that we are able to prevent abuse, we preserve our witness as a gospel-preaching church that takes sin seriously. If, God forbid, abuse does occur and it is a result of the church's negligence, our church's witness in the community is tarnished. Neighbors will know our church to be a place where abusers hurt children, rather than as a beacon of light for the good news of the gospel.

Rules, Rules, Rules!

To all this talk of policies, one might object, "If we are Christians, aren't we supposed to live by grace, and not by legalism and rules?" Absolutely! Paul makes clear in Romans 6:1–2 that grace will triumph over sin. So then, someone might say, "Why bother with a CPP? We live by grace, not the law."

The law plays an important role in the Christian life. It cannot be completely discarded. To do so would be to oversimplify Christianity. The great theologian John Calvin taught that one of the three functions of the law was its role in restraining sin. We create a CPP because we recognize there is sin in this world, because there are people who want to do evil against children, and because we have a responsibility to protect these kids. A CPP is more than just rules; it is a set of guidelines to restrain sin and to keep child abusers away from our kids.

If your church does not have a CPP, pray about it, look at Appendix A in the back of the book, and talk with your pastor about creating one. If your church does have a CPP, review it and make sure you are doing everything you can (humanly speaking) to protect and care for your kids.

CHAPTER 7

· · · ·

A Check-in and Checkout Process

Kendria was standing alongside the visitor station with a smile on her face. She was what you'd expect from a happy, welcoming church volunteer. "Are you new? Can I help you this morning?"

A visiting family had just wandered onto the children's ministry floor, and they had that "We are lost" look on their faces. They were wondering, "How do we get our children checked in to the correct classroom so we can join the rest of the adults in the worship service?"

That's a reasonable question for visitors to ask, and it prompts some further questions that we need to consider: Why do churches have check-in and checkout procedures? Why not just let the parents *informally* drop off and pick up their kids? What can we do to make sure child abusers don't get a hold of our kids? How do we guarantee that the *right* children are returned to the *right* parents?

Of the strategies discussed in this section of the book, the one addressed in this chapter probably will be the most obvious, but it still needs a bit of explaining. Churches should have a clear check-in and checkout process for children in the church. Check-in and checkout procedures create a fence around the children, allowing them to safely reside in the care of the church until they are given back to their parents.

Goals

There are three goals for any check-in and checkout process in children's ministry:

First, you want to make it clear when the child is under the care of the children's workers and when the child is being returned to the responsibility of his parents. When a parent checks his son in and hands him over to the teacher in a classroom, that moment marks the point at which the children's ministry team has officially taken responsibility for that child. When is the child no longer the responsibility of the children's ministry staff and volunteers? After the parent checks the child out and receives the child back into his or her care. Without a clear check-in process, the line of responsibility becomes fuzzy. For liability's sake alone, it is good to make this line as distinct as possible.

Second, you want to give volunteers an organized system that matches children with parents and vice versa. For example, you could use a system of numbered wrist bracelets, where one bracelet goes on each child's arm and a matching bracelet goes to the child's parent. If a volunteer were not sure if he was giving the *right* child to the *right* parent, the check-in system would provide a way of ensuring he wasn't doing something wrong.

Third, you want a system that can help you stop a child from being turned over to someone who is not the rightful guardian. Imagine if an estranged mother, who no longer has guardianship for her son because of a history of abuse, came to check him out while the foster parents were in the church service. Sound too farfetched? A church shared this real-life example with me, and it was a good test to see if their system worked. You need a system that will prevent the child from being turned over to the wrong person.

Why Isn't Informal Okay?

It is normal for most medium-to-large churches to have some type of check-in and checkout system in place, simply because they have so many kids to account for. Smaller churches tend to do a number of things informally, including how they organize children's ministry. The thinking is something like, "We're like a happy family," or "We know everybody around here, so we don't need anything formal."

It might seem silly to do anything more formal in a church with just forty or fifty people, but picture this scenario: Judy is a visiting mom, and she drops off her three-year-old son Tom at the nursery in the small Presbyterian church downtown. The volunteer (let's call her Betty) cares for Judy's son and several other young children in the church. At the end of the service a tall man comes down whom Betty has never met before, and he wants to pick up Tom. She's not sure whether or not he looks like Tom. Tom is so preoccupied with a toy spaceship that he isn't paying any attention to the man. The other kids are already picked up, and the man seems ready to get the boy and go. He doesn't seem anxious, angry, or annoyed. In fact, he is quite friendly. But the fact remains, Judy has never met this guy before, and the boy isn't exactly jumping up into his arms with great joy. What does she do? How does she know for sure that this boy belongs to this adult? If the church has kept the system informal, there is no way for Betty to know *for certain*. Something as simple as matching bracelets upon check-in and checkout could have given her all the data she needed to feel better about giving Tom over to this man—or declining to do so.

Informal check-in and checkout procedures leave too many potential problems, even in small churches where everyone supposedly knows each other. Having a formal process in place eliminates many of those problems.

Options

Again, there are a lot of practical ways to organize a check-in and checkout process—numbered wrist bands, computer-printed name tags, matching colored shirts, etc. What system you use really depends on the size of your church, what your church can afford, and if you prefer a paper system (log books, stickers, or bracelets) or a computerized system (computers, printers, touch screens, databases, parent-friendly interfaces, etc.).

Below are a few examples of companies that specialize in check-in and checkout systems:

Wristband Resources (www.wristband.com) - Provides a matching numbered and/or colored bracelet for both parent and child

Lambs List (www.lambslist.com) - Lower-cost database

KidCheck (www.kidcheck.com) - Higher-cost database

Fellowship One (www.fellowshipone.com) - A comprehensive church database, of which the children's ministry check-in is just one component

Scenarios

What should happen when kids are checked in and out of your childcare system? Here are just a few scenarios to consider:

Identity Verification

Brent was working in the four- and five-year-olds' room as a Sunday morning volunteer. A brand new member dropped her son off at the beginning of the service. When she returned at the end of the service, Brent wasn't completely sure if he recognized her. So he asked to see her identification.

"Sorry to do this," Brent began, "but I need to see your identification bracelet."

She happily held out her arm and let him read the number on the bracelet. Then he walked over to the child and asked the boy to hold out his arm. Brent checked the bracelet and saw that the number on the child's bracelet matched the mother's bracelet.

Even though he didn't need to do this, Brent also asked the boy to look up at the door and tell him who that was. The boy looked up and declared, "That's Mommy!" Now Brent was doubly sure that the *right* child was being given to the *right* adult.

Out of his discomfort, Brent could have not asked to see the bracelet, but he would have put the child's safety in jeopardy. So, to be a responsible volunteer, he made the slightly awkward request to see the bracelet. Any parent who wants their kids kept safe should happily comply with Brent's request. After all, the child was under the care of the church, and Brent had a responsibility to match the right child with the right parent. Brent was initially unsure about his actions, but he was able to rely on the check-in system to verify that he was making the correct decision regarding the identity of the parent.

Preventing Trouble

Now imagine the same scenario, but suppose the adult did not have a matching wrist bracelet upon returning from the worship service. The volunteer can say "no problem" and then give over the child. But that would be putting the child's safety in jeopardy.

In this situation, the church needs to have a way for the parent to identify himself or herself. A child protection manual I recently read gave the following option: "In the event that a parent loses their security bracelet, they will be asked to show their driver's license and the desk attendant or service coordinator will match this to the child using the computer system. The children's safety is our first priority."[1]

If the volunteer was aware of this procedure, the parent could be correctly matched up with his or her child using the computer system and a driver's license. If the church was smaller and didn't own a computerized checkout system then a picture directory of parents could be stored in the class to help volunteers properly identity the parent. If the volunteer does not know of a way to check when a parent loses a bracelet, then both parent and volunteer are stuck in an awkward situation.

Why does this even matter? We don't want a sexual offender (or really anyone) to wrongfully take a child from the church. We don't even want the wrong family member taking responsibility for a child. Remember the example of the estranged, abusive mother that I gave at the start of the chapter? She tried to trick the volunteers and check out her child while the foster parents were in the worship service. Do you think that is an isolated incident? Here's another example: A fairly large local church just told me the story of how an estranged father, who no longer had parental rights to his son, tried to check out the boy while the mother was in the main worship service. He couldn't get the child legally through their court battles, so he was trying to trick the church into giving the child over to him.

Good-Bye, Good-Bye, Good-Bye

One of the happiest moments of the day for our kids is when we get to go home after a long Sunday morning at church. Our kids have learned a lot about Jesus, they've made good friends in their classes, and they've grown attached to several of their teachers. Yet at the end of the day they are ready to return to the safe, comforting, loving arms of their mother and father.

Let's put it another way: At the end of a long Sunday morning at church, kids are tired, hungry, and ready for naps. Volunteers are exhausted from a draining morning with other people's kids. Ideally, parents are spiritually refreshed and ready to take on the challenges of a new week.

Parents want to get their kids *quickly* after a church service. Church volunteers want to return the kids *safely* to their rightful parents. And, at the end of a long but enjoyable service at church, most people want to be done and head home.

So, be kind to your church's parents, kids, and volunteers. If you don't have a clear check-in or checkout system, get one. If you don't have a good check-in or checkout procedure, get a better one. And don't leave volunteers to wonder, like Judy, whether or not to hand little Tom over to the unfamiliar man waiting at the nursery doorway.

CHAPTER 8

. . . .

MEMBERSHIP

"What do you mean I can't help right now?"

It was an awkward question, and one that deserved a response. I was standing at the door of our sanctuary, and as pastors often do after the morning service, I was talking with a visitor. My response: "We'd like you to consider joining the church *before* you throw yourself into ministries like hospitality, Angel Tree, teaching English to international students, and college ministry."

Shocking, I know. Most Christians expect to be able to volunteer *immediately* in a church *without* having to make any type of formal commitment. In our individualistic, consumer-minded society, a lot of people (maybe most) come to church with a "What's in it for me?" attitude. They don't want to make a formal commitment. To some degree, they are commitment-phobic, fearful that if they give themselves over, they'll miss out on something newer, better, greater that will be coming around the corner. They are going to stick around only as long as it works for them and they're getting what they want.

If you're like a lot of Christians, myself included, you have visited a church basically "shopping" for what you thought was best for you. Good parking? Clean bathrooms? A vibrant children's ministry? Contemporary songs that make you feel good? Traditional hymns that resonate with truth? A kind-hearted pastor whose teaching seems relevant to what you're dealing with? Small groups with people like you?

Thus, my third strategy in this section of the book might surprise you, especially since it is not usually talked about in the children's ministry world: church membership. Children's ministry coordinators are often inclined to welcome the help of any "warm body" who is capable of watching kids and at the very least regularly attends the church. So, asking them to also consider taking only church members into the children's ministry might seem a bit much, right?

Here's the reason I want to argue for church membership and why (I think) it is relevant to you: A careful, deliberate membership process can help to decrease the likelihood of sexual offenders infiltrating your children's ministry. For one thing, a church with a membership process is trying to make sure it is made up of genuine believers, and genuine believers are less likely to abuse kids. A church membership process also causes the church leaders and staff (and other members) to get to know people before they join the church, rather than giving them immediate access to the church and, consequently, the church's kids. Finally, a church membership process causes pedophiles to think twice about joining, especially since there are other churches that don't require this and will give them almost immediate access to children.

Remember, no plan is foolproof, but there are ways to reduce the risk. Church membership can help you do that by making sure those around the children are at least somewhat known entities.[1] Having asserted the importance of background checks for anyone in "regular contact with children in the church," Pastor Jared Wilson further argues, "It will also help if volunteers in [children's ministry] are required to be members of the church, assuming membership in a church entails clear communication about covenant responsibilities and church discipline."[2] On the basis of this counsel, let's talk about what I understand church membership to entail.

Church Membership

Church membership is a conscious commitment to a local body of believers who are devoted to Christ and committed to one another. It's a way of refuting the "lone-rangerism" that marks many Christians—i.e., the attitude of "I can get through the Christian life just fine on my own." It is a way to openly say, "I *can't* do this by myself." The safest and smartest thing you can do as a Christian is to partner with a local group of believers who will walk alongside you through both good times and bad.

When you think about church membership, don't think in terms of a book club or social club or membership at a local gym. A better analogy is a marriage. Just as a husband and wife commit to one another, so also you can commit to a local body of believers, walking alongside them for the sake of growing in Christ (Ephesians 4:11–16).[3]

In my denomination, there is a wide variety of ways in which a Christian can choose to join a church. Some churches allow you to just walk the aisle at the end of the service, profess faith in Christ in front of everyone, and then the pastor calls for a vote to include you right then and there. Really, it's that simple. They just need your name and your profession that you're a Christian, and basically they'll let you in.

In stark contrast, consider a church with a more extended joining process. To join, you need to go through a seven-week membership class to get to know the church better and to make sure you fully understand the leadership's expectations as you join. After completing the class, you then need to sit down for a one-hour interview with one of the pastors, where you're cross-examined about your background, your testimony, and your understanding of the gospel. The pastor is then able to assess if you're making a *credible* profession of faith that matches up with your life and testimony (Luke 6:43–46). A church's membership is supposed to be made up of *real* Christians—that is, true believers. People who don't just "talk the talk" but also "walk the walk." People who strive genuinely, albeit imperfectly, to follow Christ.

Every church is filled with imperfect Christians, banding together to help one another follow Christ. The pastor has a responsibility to guard the front door of the church, making sure those in positions of both service and leadership are genuine believers. As the church grows more and more to consist of those who genuinely follow Christ, it will look less like the world and much more like a beacon of light on a hill.

Church Membership as a Firewall

Now, which do you think a sexual offender is going to gravitate to more quickly—the low wall of the join-right-now altar-call church or the high wall of the "slow down, let's make sure you're genuinely a believer" church?

Anna Salter has said, "I do not find that most pedophiles are looking for a challenge; most are looking for an easy target."[4] If the pedophile had to climb over a low wall or a high wall, my bet is he'd choose the low wall almost every time. As we've seen so far, child abusers are very deliberate. Their goal is easy access to children. If the join-right-now church allows them to join this Sunday and be involved in children's ministry the very next week, why bother with churches that have a much longer membership process?

Because God has a heart for the lost, we want our churches to be welcoming to everyone. However, we need to balance this with wisdom regarding those who come through the front door. Anyone can come to church, but not everyone who comes should have access to our kids. Wisdom is necessary in deciding whom you allow to participate in children's ministry.

Church membership can be a firewall for children's ministry. If church membership is only for genuine believers, and if a genuine believer is much less likely ever to abuse a child, the combination of these two factors should lower the risk of abuse to our children. When pastors are careless about whom they allow into church membership, the removal of this firewall increases the risk to our kids.

These days, many church leaders are caught up in growing their churches as big and as fast as possible. For some of you, if you were to mention church membership (and maybe some type of membership class) as a criterion for service in children's ministry, the pastor would likely balk at the suggestion. If that is true for you, you might consider giving your pastor a few resources to help him think about church health (like Pastor Mark Dever's *9 Marks of a Healthy Church* or his shorter version *What Is a Healthy Church?*) or church membership (like Jonathan Leeman's *Church Membership: How The World Knows Who Represents Jesus* or his much longer volume *The Church and the Surprising Offense of God's Love*).

Don't get frustrated if a stronger emphasis on membership doesn't seem to be an option in your situation. If that's the case, you can still implement some type of screening process for working with children that will make the front door of children's ministry smaller. Some ideas to shrink the door might include the following:

- A brief interview with the children's ministry director before volunteers are accepted. This gives the director a chance to get to know the person before granting access to the kids.
- An application process that includes screening and reference checks on volunteers.
- A required training seminar for all volunteers.
- A six-month waiting period after they've arrived at the church and before they are given access to children.

In the 1990s, when the scandals of Catholic priests abusing children dominated the news, many church insurance companies responded by mandating a six-month waiting period for new members or regular attenders before they were allowed to work with children. This was intended to slow down prospective members enough so that the church could get to know them better *before* they were granted access to children.

The point of all these measures is not to give anyone—leaders *or* volunteers—immediate access to children. This simple guideline would not have prevented many of the tragic incidents that occurred in the Catholic church, but it could have saved *some* kids who had been put under the care of a sexual offender who had just joined the church.

How *Well* Do You Know Them?

The obvious question to ask is: How well do you know your volunteers? The bigger the church, the harder it is to know everybody. But even in small churches, familiarity can breed false assumptions about how well you truly know a person.

A thoughtful church membership process is a way to help consumeristic, lone-ranger Christians give up their selfishness and commit themselves to the hard work of walking alongside other believers. As we've seen, in regard to sexual offenders, it is also a way of giving your church the time it needs to get to know new people *before* they start spending time with the children.

Admittedly, anything that slows down the process of integrating volunteers in your children's ministry tangibly amounts to fewer volunteers helping, particularly in the short term. But it's a small price to pay when it comes to protecting our kids. Membership, screening and training, and a six-month waiting period all increase the likelihood that you'll actually know the people who work with your kids—and also help ensure that the people who go through this process really *do* care about your children.

CHAPTER 9

· · · ·

SCREENING AND VERIFICATION

"I lied to you."

I hate these four words. They haven't come often in my life, but every time it's happened, it's frustrated me that I didn't detect the lie. After all, I'm a professional counselor by training. I spend my days sorting through sin and sifting through people's personal issues. Of all people, I should be able to tell if someone's lying, right?

Wrong. Professionals who work with sexual offenders make four things very clear[1]:

1. People are not good at detecting lying.
2. People *think* they are good at detecting lying.
3. The things that most people believe will help them detect deception won't.
4. The things that will signal deception are subtle, easy to miss, and not well known.

Although most people believe they can naturally detect lying, decades of research demonstrate that people cannot reliably tell who is telling the truth and who is not.

Child abusers build their whole lives around lying. They put on the persona of a nice guy just to get access to children—to earn their trust (and sometimes that of a church community) so that they can repeatedly abuse those children. You might think you'll be able to

spot this if it happens in your church, but the success of sexual offenders—many of whom abuse dozens of kids—shows that most of
the time they will get away with it long before anyone figures them
out.

So, what are we to do? How do we protect our kids? Our in-
ability to detect lying points us to the fourth strategy: screening and
verification. Most sexual offenders assume churches won't check
up on them—and most churches, in fact, do not. If they did, they
would find a trail of hurt children and ruined lives. But too many
child abusers continue offending because churches don't do their due
diligence in verifying and screening staff and volunteers.

One of the most important steps in protecting against sexual
offenders is implementing a system of screening and verification procedures that will detect when an abuser is prowling around your
church. You are trying to make sure a person's words and actions line
up with one another. It's not safe to assume that because a staff member or volunteer is a self-professing Christian, that person is okay to
work with kids.

In order to have an effective screening and verification process, a
church will want to consider a number of tools, including a written
application, references, interview, background check, and possibly
fingerprinting. A successful screening and verification program depends on employing a multi-faceted approach, and not just one or
two of these means.[2] I recommend all of these things to help your
church verify that there are no skeletons in a person's closet and no
criminal behavior in his past.

Screening

Screening begins with information provided by the potential staff
member or volunteer—a written application that includes sensitive
questions related to difficult areas of sin and suffering as well as references and a personal interview.

The Written Application

Along with your basic, entry-level children's ministry training (see Chapter 11 for more information on training), you can ask staff and volunteers to fill out some type of written application as a part of your screening. Why? An application allows the church to document its efforts in screening and selecting staff and volunteers, and it demonstrates the church's desire to maintain reasonable care of its children through the careful selection of its personnel and volunteers.[3]

The application should ask for the following:

- Basic data about the person (name, phone number, address, email, etc., including an indication of whether the person is age eighteen or older);
- Family information (single, married, divorced status; names and ages of any children);
- Current church membership or regular attender information (When did you join or start attending? What if any other ministries are you involved in?);
- Prior church membership;
- Past experiences in helping children or youth;
- Several references from previous churches or your current church;
- Sensitive questions related to a person's background (discussed below); and
- Consent to do a background check, including criminal background and social media checks.

For those interested in more details about the application, an example is included in Appendix D of this book.

Who should fill out this application? Any adult serving in children's ministry, usually meaning someone age eighteen or older. If there are teenagers helping in children's ministry programs, a screening process should be undertaken. This is essential in part because of the increasing prevalence of child-on-child abuse (see Appendix B for more on this problem). However, it is the church's decision whether to apply the same or different standards in questioning teenagers.[4]

Reference Checks

Collecting at least two references allows the church to connect with people from the applicant's past and check on his or her previous experiences with children. Former employers, colleagues, close friends, pastors, small-group leaders, or mentors can all serve as good references. Relatives or close blood relations should not be accepted as references, especially since family members can be less willing to report one another's unethical behavior.[5]

The children's ministry director can send references a list of questions like the following:

- How long have you known [name], and in what capacity?
- Describe his/her character.
- Has he/she ever given you cause to doubt his/her personal integrity?
- What are his/her spiritual strengths?
- What are his/her weaknesses?
- Do you have any hesitations or concerns whatsoever about [name] working closely with children or youth in a church setting?
- Is there anyone else you would encourage us to contact?

You might think, "Who is going to give you a bad reference?" If they want to work with kids, they'll give you the names of people who think highly of them. Generally speaking, that might be true, but I've been surprised how often a reference check will bring something of concern to our attention simply because the person on the other end was very honest with us. But even if most references come back positive, the point is to actually take the time to check. Remember, child abusers assume you won't. Taking the time to check proves to them that your church isn't like most others that don't bother checking on their staff and volunteers.

As a part of the screening application, it is important to include a waiver for the church and the person providing the reference. If the reference knows that the person being screened has granted to her a release from liability, it allows her to be even more honest without fear of repercussions for her honesty.[6]

Sensitive Questions

Included in the application is a list of sensitive questions about the applicant's life. These questions allow the church to ask the person directly about sin struggles and suffering (current or past) that might compromise his or her ability to work with children. On your application, you might include questions like these:

- Have you ever been a victim of abuse?
- Have you ever been accused of, participated in, pled guilty to, or been convicted of child abuse, child neglect, or any other crime against a minor?
- Have you ever been convicted of or pled guilty to any crime (other than minor traffic violations)?
- Have you deliberately and repeatedly viewed pornography in the past three years?
- Have you ever participated in homosexual conduct?
- Do you have any communicable diseases or infections such as tuberculosis, Hepatitis B, HIV/AIDS, MRSA, etc.?
- Have you ever, or do you now, struggle with drunkenness?
- Have you ever, or do you now, struggle with some kind of addiction?

Every congregation has different struggles, depending on the demographics of the congregation and the location of the church. With our congregation in downtown Washington, DC, there are a lot of struggles with pornography and marital conflict, but very little drug addiction or alcoholism. In a congregation on an American Indian reservation, the dominant sin is often drunkenness, while a church in India will face a society plagued with frequent rape of women. So, depending on where you live, the list of sensitive questions on the application will need to change to fit the common sins of your congregation and cultural context.

Most of the data on the application is not sensitive (address, phone, email, etc.), but the data on this last page of the application should be handled with great care because of its delicate nature. It should be given only to those who need to know, such as a pastor or a godly, mature staff member.[7] The pastor reviews the answers and calls the volunteer whenever the applicant answers "yes" or "I would like to discuss" to any of these questions. The goal is to screen the person out of children's ministry if their sin might inhibit their ability to properly care for the children in the church. For example, someone who has been abused is more likely to abuse. Therefore, we need to ask explicit questions about past abuse. Or, if someone has been convicted of a crime (or a number of crimes), you know that they have been willing to ethically compromise themselves, so you probably don't want to entrust them with care of your children.

A lot of pastoral wisdom is needed to decide if applicants are adequately dealing with their sin and suffering, such that they can be competent and caring childcare workers or teachers of children. A few questions you might ask yourself: Are they repentant of sin and fighting for faith? Do I see them acting responsibly in the different parts of their lives? Are they humble, teachable, and responsive to God's Word and God's people? Are they striving for unity within the congregation and supportive of the church's leadership?

I would be more inclined to use someone in children's ministry who is actively fighting sin, is living out faith (albeit imperfectly), is actively involved in the church, is well-known by others, and is supportive of the church's leaders. In contrast, I'd be less inclined to use someone in a children's ministry setting who is new to the church, is not well-known, is in unrepentant sin or struggling with a besetting sin, and/or claims to be a Christian but is not showing evidence of it.

As the staff member who has done countless phone calls to children's ministry applicants, many of these pastoral conversations have turned into wonderful opportunities to care for a struggling Christian in our congregation. So, as you do the screening call, don't just think defensively (e.g., How do we protect our kids?), but proactively (e.g., How can I use this opportunity to shepherd this person through his sin or suffering?). Children's ministry volunteers should be treated as more than just a warm body who watches kids; they should be treated as image-bearers who have value and dignity in the eyes of God. You should treat them in the same way that God treats all of us—with undeserved grace and mercy (Luke 15:11–32; Romans 5:9; Ephesians 2:5–8). Don't just use your volunteers to get the job done; shepherd them and care for their souls.

The Interview

Most experts encourage churches to incorporate some kind of personal interview into their screening process. From one church to another the types of workers asked to go through a personal interview will differ, depending on the church's size and number of children's ministry volunteers. If the church's size allows for staff to do personal interviews of all members who come in contact with children, this allows for a careful screening of everyone. For very large churches with hundreds of volunteers, this level of screening may not be possible. In this case, interviews would be limited to key leaders in children's ministry or anyone who has the potential to be in more one-on-one settings with children, such as disciplers or mentors.

The interview should deal with a variety of topics, ranging from spiritual conversion to abuse prevention. It will be important *to get a sense of the person's general well-being and spiritual state.* Are they doing well spiritually and growing in their faith? Are they actively fighting sin? Do they enjoy being a part of the church? If a person is doing poorly in their personal or spiritual life (either because of besetting sins or ongoing suffering), it could hinder their ability to care for children or to communicate truth to them.

It will also be good to talk with the person about their responsibilities, if they have time to carry out their responsibilities, and what they would enjoy about this role. In our experience, those who are forced to do something will be less reliable, in contrast to those who come to it of their own initiative with a servant's heart and an eagerness to help.

It is good to ask why the person wants to work with children. Because sexual offenders tend to be egocentric, their responses can at times revolve around the good that the child can do for them rather than the good that the adult can do for the child. We want to distinguish between those who expect the children to meet their needs and those who volunteer for children's ministry in order to serve the children.[8]

If this person is taking on a leadership role in children's ministry (either as staff or a key volunteer), it is important to see if the person is going to support the church's leaders and work toward building unity within the church body. The church leadership saves itself from some conflict and turmoil by screening out those who are going to be potentially divisive later on.

It is vital to review the child protection policy (CPP), to see if the person has any reluctance in following these guidelines. Someone who expresses reluctance in the interview is certainly less likely to follow through in a real-life situation.[9]

One way to help make sure the person understands the CPP is to give him a few scenarios and ask him how he might respond. Include one or two situations related to preventing or responding to abuse. Help the volunteer to think about how the policies work out in real life, and again assess his willingness to respond according to the guidelines. See Appendix F for examples of scenarios that you can use in an interview or volunteer training.

Check to see if the person has adult friendships. Experts warn that a church should not entrust its children to an adult who doesn't have healthy adult friendships but instead consistently gravitates toward children's settings. Anna Salter says that churches should "be careful with men who involved themselves in youth activities and who do not have children of their own or children of that age. From church youth leaders to coaches to anyone who befriends your child, notice if they have grown-up friends and partners. If they do not, be very cautious about leaving them alone with your child."[10]

An interview is not foolproof. Sexual offenders are very practiced at lying, so they will often know how to give the "right" answers. But the simple act of conducting an interview communicates that the church is serious about protecting children—and that fact alone will scare some offenders away. Even if the interview doesn't stop a sexual offender, it will likely screen out some folks who will not be reliable volunteers for children's ministry.[11]

Verification

Why wouldn't these four measures just discussed—written application, references, sensitive questions about sin and suffering, and an interview—be enough? Up to this point, the information provided is dependent on what the applicant is willing to reveal to you. You don't have anything that goes beyond their answers or their self-submitted references. All of these steps are essentially *self-authenticating*. If someone was committed to deceiving and lying to the church community, it wouldn't take much for him to fool others about sin from his past. He can lie—or get others to lie for him. That's why it's important to go beyond the self-authenticating information provided by applicants and to verify their stories using outside sources of information. The two ways to do this are background checks and fingerprinting.

Background Checks

Criminal background checks allow the church to use law enforcement and other government databases to check on a person's background. There also are Internet services available for free and private screening companies that will conduct a thorough background check for a fee.

Two examples of private screening companies that conduct criminal background checks are Protect My Ministry (www.protect

myministry.com) and Secure Search (www.securesearchpro.com). These professional screening companies cost money, but there is a menu of options and a varied price range depending on how extensive a search you want to conduct. Typically, you can purchase a fairly thorough screening at about twenty to thirty dollars per person.

Criminal background checks can include county, state, multistate, or national checks. National checks are either checks into individual state databases, checks run through a centralized database like the Department of Justice public sex offender registry, or both. County checks are considered to be the most accurate because they contain court convictions and orders that may or may not be shown in the state or federal databases. The problem with a county check is that it is geographically limited; the offender might live in one county but have committed a crime in another county. A single-county check won't show the crime performed in a neighboring county, so the effectiveness of county checks is increased by doing searches in multiple counties.[12] And, because thirty-eight percent of repeat sexual offenses take place in areas other than where the previous offense was committed, experts also advise churches to do multistate and national checks alongside the county checks.[13] The best combination of criminal background checks will include queries into multistate and national databases as well as in one to three counties where the applicant has previously lived.

Someone might ask, "Is a criminal background check really necessary? It seems a bit extreme." Ideally, criminal background checks will be done for everyone who volunteers with children. We give three reasons why we think this is a good standard for churches. First, many children and youth service organizations mandate criminal background checks for their staff and volunteers, and in this case churches should take their lead. Why would churches, who place a much higher value on children because of our biblical values, want to create a lower standard of protection and care than secular organizations? Second, churches that mandate criminal background checks for all volunteers would be in a much better position to defend themselves in court against accusations of negligence.[14] Third, criminal background checks also reveal other types of behavior that might disqualify a staff member or volunteer from working with children or youth, like domestic violence, drunk driving, weapons violations, etc.[15]

If doing background checks for all staff and volunteers is not possible for a church, at the very least such checks should be required for all who have leadership roles or discipling/mentoring roles in children's or youth ministry. Authors James Cobble, Richard Hammer, and Steven Klipowicz argue that criminal background checks are warranted in the event of extended one-on-one contact with minors or frequent and unsupervised contact with minors. They suggest that such checks may not be needed in settings with multiple adults if there is infrequent, indirect contact with minors or contact in group settings.[16] I would argue for a higher standard: If it is financially possible, the church should do a criminal background check on *all* staff and volunteers, regardless of their official or expected degree of contact with children.

If your church can't afford a more extensive criminal background check, pick a level of screening that fits your church budget, and adjust the background check based on the person's profile. For example, in our church, men get a more extensive screening than women and single men a more extensive screening than married men. Why? A more intense background check for men in general and single men in particular is based on our knowledge that sexual offenders are primarily men and often times single. We strongly recommend that everyone who comes in contact with children should get some type of criminal background check.

If your church can't afford to employ a professional screening service, then consider using a few of the free websites like the Justice Department's national sexual offenders registry (www.nsopr.gov). Just keep in mind that the offenders listed on these sites are men who have been tried, convicted, *and have taken the time to register their most recent address.* If someone has never been convicted, has evaded registering in his community, or is currently on trial in a local court, that person won't show up on any sexual offender website. Free websites provide some helpful data, but there will be limitations on what they can provide for you. Therefore, if at all possible, we encourage churches *not* to use a free sex offender registry as a *substitute* for a criminal background check. These free registries are notorious for their inaccuracies, and offenders sometimes fail to update their information.[17]

If a church only does a criminal background check and doesn't employ any other means of screening or verification, it can lead to a false sense of security. The absence of convictions from a criminal background check does not definitively prove that a person is not an abuser. It may just show that he or she has not been caught. Since criminal background checks typically only reveal convictions, they should not be a substitute for actually *knowing* the people that you put in positions of responsibility with children.[18]

With the vast array of social media outlets that have developed over the last few years, a lot of data can also be gathered by doing online searches or viewing social media websites such as Facebook, LinkedIn, Instagram, or Twitter. The simplest way to conduct an online search is to type a person's name into a search engine like Google and see what links come up. To view a person's social media sites, in many cases it will be necessary to obtain the person's permission to view his or her online profile. But if this person plans to serve in children's ministry, the church can decide if it wants to make such permission a requirement for service. In the case of large churches, it probably will not be feasible for staff to spend a lot of time doing social media background checks; they might consider employing one of any number of social media screening services now available to assist churches.

Fingerprinting

Fingerprinting is the most thorough way of finding a child abuser. It provides access to the widest spectrum of agencies that deal with sexual offenders, and it is thorough enough to be a substitute for criminal background checks.[19]

That said, fingerprinting is also the most expensive and invasive means of verification available. I typically recommend that it be used for situations where someone will have extensive and/or unsupervised access to children or youth, such as someone whose role allows him or her to spend significant one-on-one time with a child or teenager, such as a discipler or mentor.

Checking on Church Staff

Every church employee should undergo some kind of screening and verification as a part of the church's hiring process. The extent of the screening and verification will depend on the staff member's job responsibilities. A children's ministry director or a youth leader should be more extensively scrutinized than the preaching pastor or the building janitor, but all four should be checked.[20]

There are a number of abuse cases where the abuse occurred at the hands of a church employee who was not serving on the children's ministry or youth staff. If a church employee abuses a child, and the church is taken to court, the church will be cross-examined regarding its hiring practices. Churches can't expect preferential treatment but should expect to be held to the same standard of care as other organizations that work with children.[21] Churches should desire excellence in all that they do and should be an example in our society of the best standard of care for children. Yet, because of laziness and carelessness, they often are the worst examples.[22]

Don't let your church set a bad example. The simplest and most basic thing a church can do is to make sure that all employees undergo a criminal background check as a part of the hiring process. If a check brings up any evidence of past criminal behavior, it should have immediate implications for hiring.

Obstacles to Screening and Verification

Church members and staff who are not used to screening or verification procedures are likely to be surprised by these suggestions. In an age where identity theft is common, people will be reluctant to give away so much personal information on an application. Others will consider background checks or fingerprinting as an invasion of privacy. Since children's ministries are often desperate for volunteers, leaders will be concerned about these procedures scaring people away.[23] They might deem these measures as unnecessary, since the church is small and family-like. However, familiarity often breeds contentment and decreases our vigilance in checking on people. Maybe folks will be willing to fill out the application but will balk when they see the sensitive questions at the back of the application. They might ask, "Why do we need to answer this if we're working with children?" or "Isn't this a little too personal?"

Forcing a church to do these things is a futile venture. To make this work, you need to prepare the congregation *before* any of these means are employed. Getting leadership to see the value of this and sign off is a crucial first step. The church can't really change its practices unless the leadership is behind the change. Once that happens, a systemic process of educating the congregation should ensue. Training events for new and old volunteers will help educate members on the value of screening and verification. Once people understand the value of these things, there will be less resistance. Your overall goal is to help this to become a *normal* expectation in your church—that all members should be screened and verified before working with kids. No exceptions allowed.

The first time you get everyone screened and verified in your church will be hard. You'll face a lot of obstacles and pushback as you try to make this a normal practice. But once you get beyond the initial season of screening and verification, it should get easier as these procedures become an expected part of serving in children's ministry.

Make This Permanent, Not Just a Passing Fad

If a child advocate convinces a church to do screening for a time but leaves afterward, the church will often slack off on its screening and verification procedures. The advocate has left behind a church that is less enthusiastic and has less motivation to follow through with the work that needs to be done. What helps these procedures to be sustained over time?

Again, the church's leadership needs to be supportive. These practices should be incorporated into the church's children's ministry policy. As a part of that policy, an updated check should be scheduled every three to five years for each person, so that this is not just a one-time event. And implementation of these checks should be assigned to a staff member or lead volunteer as part of his or her job responsibilities.

Lie Detector Tests?

It would be rather awkward to ask every member of your church to take a lie detector test. I don't expect that they would want to come back the next week for fear of what you might do next! Short of having a lie detector available, what else can we do? Experts say that the most common ways that perpetual liars are detected are when they self-contradict or when an outside source verifies that they are telling a lie.[24]

It is hard to catch a sex offender's self-contradictions because they don't do it all that often. Therefore, it's important to screen and verify children's ministry workers. We've considered a few ways to catch a sex offender—a written application that gathers references and data on sensitive questions, a personal interview, employing professional screening services to check on a person's background, verifying information through social-media outlets, and fingerprinting. We employ each of these procedures because, by ourselves, we are unlikely to detect a liar when he comes across our path. We need help to verify that his words are truthful and his life is not disingenuous.

Do you know whether the volunteers and staff in your church have been screened and verified by some of the means we described in this chapter? If you don't know, ask your pastor, children's ministry director, or youth minister. You don't want to be a parent who is caught by surprise, like Laura Jordan was.

"I am outraged," said Laura, who attended a church with her husband and children until 2011. Earlier that year, allegations emerged against the choir director that he had raped a sixteen-year-old girl in the congregation. To make matters worse, according to the police report, the lead pastor knew that the choir director had a criminal background.[25] "The fact [is] that this pastor knew his past and he didn't let any of us know," Jordan said. "[As parents we want to know] so that we can make the decision whether to put our babies around this person."

Don't be caught off guard like Laura and her husband. Talk to your pastor and children's ministry director, and make sure they are doing everything they can to screen and verify staff and volunteers in your church. Do everything you can to protect the children that God has put under your care.

CHAPTER 10

. . . .

BUILDING DESIGN

In our church building that is one hundred years old and has five floors, it is not always obvious where to find something, and directional questions frequently arise. "Where do the Sunday school classes meet?" "Is this the sanctuary?" "Can you point me to the ladies' restroom?" And, as you might expect, "Where do I take my kids?" We get the pleasure of helping visitors navigate through the maze of our wonderful church building.

Building layout, and the structural setup of your children's ministry wing, may not be the most obvious sphere for strategizing on the prevention of sexual abuse. And it's probably the thing you can least change in your church. Yet if you've never considered it, there may in fact be simple adjustments (or larger ones) you can make to help the children in your church be safer and more secure.

Earlier in this book, we described two types of sexual predators—*power* predators, who use sheer force to abduct and overtake their victims, and *persuasion* predators, who put on a fake persona in order to get access to children. Most of our time has been focused on the persuasion predator because he will be more prevalent and more likely to try to get into a church. This chapter considers how we can better guard against the power predator. What do we do to prevent a kid from being snatched and taken away? How do we safeguard our classrooms and meeting areas so that parents don't have to worry?

How do we stop children from wandering in the wrong places? How do we set up our children's ministry wing to keep separate those who should have access to the kids (approved staff and volunteers) and those who should not (strangers or other folks wandering around)?

Three Goals

We desire three things in our children's ministry wing. First, we want *clear boundaries* that "fence in" the kids and approved volunteers and keep out those who should not have access to the kids. Clear boundaries will lead to natural divisions of space between these two groups.

Second, we want to make sure there are *no isolated areas* in our children's department. Is there a space in a classroom where an adult and a child can be without anyone else around? Is a children's class or activity set up in a place that is too far away from the rest of the church's activities? Is there a remote room or setup that makes an adult more secluded with children? If we can answer "yes" to any of these questions, we want to get rid of that classroom or setup in our children's ministry wing.

Third, we want to make sure there is *unobstructed visibility* into all of the children's classrooms. If a teacher or volunteer can shut a door and no one can see what's going on inside, we've put our children in jeopardy. Simple things, such as adding a line of sight into all the classrooms, will make the church a safer place for children.

Many years ago, when I started a job as a church secretary, the very first request I got was to add Dutch doors (picture a normal, full-size door cut in half) to our children's nursery. The youngest children had been able simply to wander out of the classrooms, and strangers could too easily walk in without anyone stopping them. One of the handymen in our church found a few extra doors sitting around in our church, cut them in half, and then hooked them up to the entrance of every nursery room. It was remarkable what a difference just a few half-doors made for keeping the approved childcare workers in and everyone else out.

Three Structural Setups

Three kinds of structural setups frequently characterize churches. I'll break these down into what I consider the ideal, the second best option, and the worst option. The building designs considered below are particularly for the youngest children (zero to five years of age) because those children are the most vulnerable in our church.

The Ideal Setup

The ideal setup involves walls that separate the entire children's ministry wing from the rest of the church and a centralized check-in desk, which all volunteers and children must pass through.

Anyone looking at this setup immediately gets the message: "You are not getting in here without passing through check-in first."

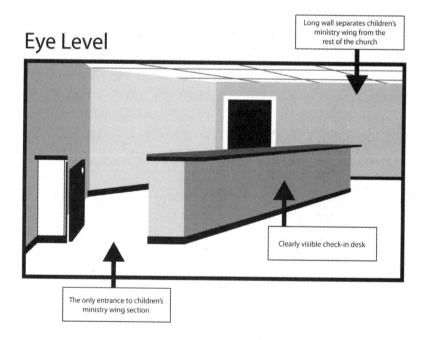

Eye Level

Long wall separates children's ministry wing from the rest of the church

Clearly visible check-in desk

The only entrance to children's ministry wing section

Aerial View

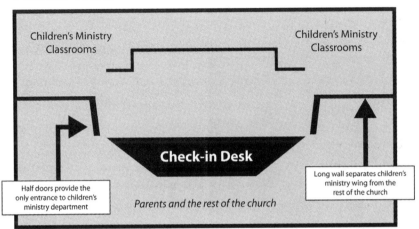

Children's Ministry Classrooms

Children's Ministry Classrooms

Check-in Desk

Half doors provide the only entrance to children's ministry department

Parents and the rest of the church

Long wall separates children's ministry wing from the rest of the church

The Second Best Option

Our next best option would be a long hallway with classrooms that are marked off with half-doors (e.g., Dutch doors) at the entrance to every classroom. The half-door option allows you to put a boundary between the parents in the hallway and the teachers and children in the class-room. It also provides considerable visibility if the top half of the door is left open.

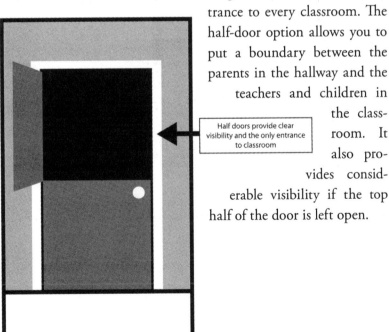

Half doors provide clear visibility and the only entrance to classroom

The Worst Option

The worst option is an unobstructed doorway where children (especially the youngest) or any adults can walk in or out—or a door that can be shut with no line of sight directly into the classroom.

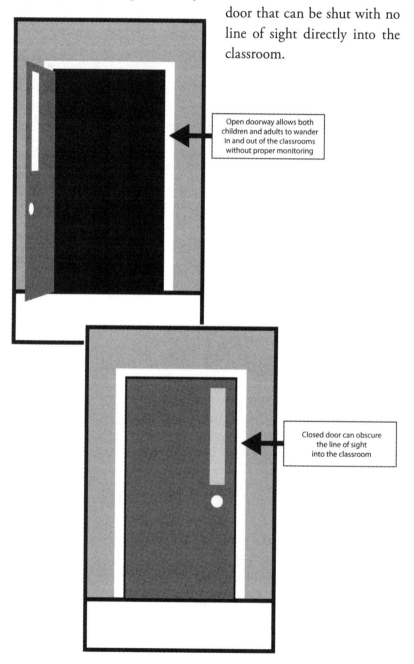

Open doorway allows both children and adults to wander in and out of the classrooms without proper monitoring

Closed door can obscure the line of sight into the classroom

Your Frustrations

You might look at these pictures and think, "What am I going to do? I'm stuck with the worst setup!" In an ideal world, the church administrator would call a few minutes from now and say to you, "A millionaire just called and donated enough money to redesign the whole children's ministry wing. So, how would you like to change everything?" Okay, so maybe this is a far-fetched dream, but never fear. Even if you don't have an ideal setup, there are often small adjustments that can be made to improve it. In my earlier example, we had a handyman cut the full doors into half-doors to keep children in and improve visibility into each classroom. Some of you might simply add larger glass panes in your doors to improve the line of sight.

If the church does undergo a building renovation, you should think of that as an opportunity to redesign your children's ministry wing in a way to make it safer for the children and more difficult for power predators to get access. An experienced architect can help you think through structural design so that you can help your kids be better protected. Some natural questions to consider would be: Is the children's ministry wing close enough for easy access for families but not residing right at the center of the main flow of traffic in your church? Is your structural setup in any way making church kids vulnerable to strangers? Are there simple changes that can be made that improve our setup but are not very expensive?

God's House of Refuge

In Scripture, God is often described as a place of refuge, strength, and safety.

> God is our refuge and strength,
>   an ever-present help in trouble.
> Therefore we will not fear, though the earth give way
>   and the mountains fall into the heart of the sea.
> (Psalm 46:1–2)

The last thing we want is to make the house of God a place where children are especially vulnerable. Adjusting or reorganizing your building design and classroom setups can be a simple way to make our children safer.

CHAPTER 11

. . . .

TRAINING YOUR STAFF AND VOLUNTEERS

"Who can take the kids to the bathroom?"

"What time am I supposed to arrive?"

"Are the kids allowed to have snacks, and, if so, what can I feed them?"

"What do we do if we're going away on the weekend that I'm scheduled to serve?"

"How do I know which kid belongs to which parent?"

"What if I suspect a child is abused or is being neglected by his parents?"

If you work in children's ministry, you're probably very familiar with questions like these and many, many others. You may struggle to adequately train the staff and volunteers who serve in the church every Sunday. How are they to know what they are supposed to do and not do? Some of your workers will figure things out by common sense, but for the most part, in order to care for the children in your church, you need to help the children's ministry staff and volunteers by telling them what they need to know.

In regard to sexual offenders and child abuse, volunteers will have a lot of questions. Because most church members develop much of their knowledge about abuse from news accounts and stereotypes, myths need to be debunked and replaced with accurate and reliable knowledge about the problem.

The training process developed below will deal much more generally with children's ministry and the variety of ways volunteers need to be equipped. But within that more general training, the church should have very specific training about abuse prevention, reporting, and response. Equip staff and volunteers so they can care well for the children of the church.

Building a Training Process

What does training look like? Think in terms of two levels: entry-level training and ongoing training. Catch new staff or volunteers as they get involved in children's ministry for the first time and then continue to equip and educate them as they stay involved.

Entry-Level Training

Entry-level training is a basic level of training that equips everyone who helps with children's ministry. The basic question we're answering is, "What do the staff and volunteers need to know to do their job faithfully?" What we don't want to do is ask staff and volunteers to come, bore them to death with a long list of basic policies and procedures, and then set them loose in the wild and crazy world of children's ministry. Here are a few things you might want to talk about with new staff and volunteers to equip them more thoroughly:

A vision for children's ministry. In the midst of diapers and temper tantrums, reading books and teaching curriculum, it's easy to lose sight of the forest for the trees. It's important to give your volunteers a sense of the bigger picture. Give them a vision for what they are doing and why they are helping. Teach them about God's glory, the blessings of children, the responsibility to pass on truth, and the hope of children becoming Christians. Don't just make them change diapers; inspire them to communicate truth and love the church's children wisely.

Childhood evangelism. Churches will differ in their approaches to evangelism of the kids, but in the end—no matter what methodology you adopt—we're all in agreement that we want to see our kids come to know Christ (John 3) and faithfully follow him for the rest of their lives (Jude 1:20–22). So it's important to help staff and volunteers to understand how to communicate the gospel effectively to children.

Classroom expectations. This ranges from classroom management ("What do I do if a child hits another kid?") to classroom activities ("Am I just entertaining the kids?") and pedagogy ("How do we teach the curriculum effectively to children?").

Policies and procedures. This has the potential to be the most boring part of your training. Who wants to spend an hour listening to a bunch of policies and procedures? But in many ways it can be the most important thing you do because these guidelines shape and define the environment that will keep the children safe. You'll need to educate them about more general policy matters, like check-in and checkout procedures, sickness policy, food and drink guidelines, appropriate discipline, evacuation and emergency procedures, etc. To communicate this effectively, make sure your volunteer trainer is engaging in his or her presentation and use some active-learning strategies, like role playing or discussions about practical scenarios.

Abuse and child neglect. The following are some basic questions that staff and volunteers need to consider in regard to abuse and neglect:

- What do I do if I suspect or observe that a child has been physically, emotionally, or sexually abused?
- Who is the point of contact at church if I suspect or witness abuse?
- What responsibility do I have to report child abuse and neglect to the police or Child Protective Services (CPS)?
- Are there common characteristics of sexual offenders for which I can be on the alert?
- What happens if a child touches me inappropriately?

- How will the church respond to allegations or admission of child abuse?
- How can I best minister to a child who has been abused or neglected?
- What additional care is required for a child who is in foster care?
- How can I guard myself from accusations?
- What happens if a sexual offender starts attending our church?

An example of a training handout that equips volunteers to think about child abuse prevention, reporting, and response has been included in Appendix E.

An important goal of this training is to develop a *healthy* level of skepticism among the staff and volunteers. You don't want your staff or volunteers to make false assumptions about child abusers but to be vigilant about protecting kids at all times.

What kind of skepticism is healthy? You don't want to make your workers paranoid that there's a sexual predator lurking behind every corner, but you don't want to carelessly assume that just because someone is a self-professing Christian, it is safe to give him or her responsibility for your church's kids.

Take, for example, a situation that might not faze you the first time or may not even bother your volunteers if it is repeated. Jonathan is a nice, single guy, and he has been around the church for several years. He comes to church regularly and has a few friendships in the church. Last week, when a child needed to be taken to the restroom, Jonathan volunteered to help. Now, that might not set off any alarm bells for you. It doesn't necessarily have to because Jonathan might be standing in front of a kid screaming at the top of his lungs that he has to go potty or he's going to have an accident. Most adults will rush a kid to the bathroom in that situation. Nothing to worry about, right?

But what if the childcare training made very clear that *only* *women* are to take children to the bathroom? More suspicious now, right? If it only happened once, then it doesn't seem like a big deal. Jonathan might have reacted quickly out of sheer fear of a screaming four-year-old who is about to wet his pants. But if Jonathan repeatedly takes young kids to the restroom and ignores the rules . . . well, then your alarm bells should go off. You shouldn't pass this off and say, "He must have just forgotten about the rule." Your healthy skepticism should lead you to say something.

If a volunteer senses something might be wrong, the last thing he should do is dismiss it or ignore it. He should be wise and sensitive to the Holy Spirit's direction as he thinks about what happened and how he should respond.

Ongoing Training

Ongoing training, by definition, means continuing to equip the volunteers as they help out in children's ministry. Practically, this might include the following:

- Helping teachers know how to manage a classroom;
- Assisting teachers in thinking about how to communicate truth in fun and developmentally appropriate ways, while making sure they don't water down the truth;
- Giving refreshers on policies and procedures because volunteers are bound to forget;
- Helping volunteers understand how to make the best use of the classroom resources;
- Helping everyone think about how to teach the gospel and live it out in front of kids; and, of course . . .
- Giving refreshers on abuse and neglect.

When volunteers are actually doing the work of caring for the kids, they'll see and understand and engage in a way that makes things much more real—which will probably prompt more questions. Find ways to engage volunteers while they are doing the good work of caring for and protecting the children in your church.

A Little Knowledge Goes a Long Way

Train your staff and children's ministry volunteers well, and you'll go a long way to reducing the risk of child abuse occurring in your church. While it takes some work to teach children's ministry workers all of these things, a healthy level of skepticism is sometimes hard to instill. But, unlike children's ministry volunteers, some people learn to be skeptics simply because of what they do for work.

Don is a sheriff in a small town in Mississippi. He's seen enough criminals and crime to be suspicious when something doesn't seem right. When Bob—a divorced adult in his forties—showed up at their little Methodist church and immediately volunteered to help with the kids, Don was suspicious. The problem was that no one else was suspicious. Don talked with the pastor, but all he got back was, "Stop being so paranoid. The county pays you to be suspicious out there, but you don't have to be like that at church." So Don did some snooping around. As he looked at a host of websites, he found out rather quickly that Bob was a convicted sex offender.

No one had suspected, except the local town sheriff. Then again, he's paid to develop an instinct for this kind of thing. Most of us don't have the benefit of having a sheriff snooping around and checking on folks in our church.

Train your volunteers and teachers. Equip them by debunking their assumptions about sexual offenders. Assist them to think through how to care for abused kids. Teach your folks to have a healthy skepticism. Don't wait around for the sheriff to do some snooping.

CHAPTER 12

. . . .

PREPARING CHURCH LEADERS, PARENTS, CHILDREN, AND TEENS *BEFORE* ABUSE HAPPENS

"I just wish I had known."

Jessica was crying. Her husband Barry sat next to her, holding his wife tightly. Their daughter Dina had been molested by a man in the church. Dina was just one in the long trail of teenagers that Jimmy had hurt. It took months before Dina owned up to her parents about what happened, and even then it was only because she had heard rumors in the youth group about the same thing happening to other girls in the church. Dina had realized that if she didn't say anything Jimmy would continue to hurt girls in the church, so she courageously spoke up and told her parents.

Could Jessica and Barry's church have helped them *before* the abuse happened? Too often, churches start figuring out how to deal with abuse *after* bad stuff happens. Their approach to the problem of child abuse is *reactive* rather than *proactive and deliberate*.

In our previous chapter, we thought about how to train and prepare children's ministry staff and volunteers who work with children. In this chapter, we'll consider a seventh strategy in preventing abuse: preparing the rest of the church—church leaders, parents, children, and teens—before evil strikes.

How do we help equip *all* of our church body to deal with abuse? What kind of leadership makes a difference? What should parents teach their children and teens in order to prevent abuse? What kind of church culture should we cultivate? What does it look like for a church to take the problem of abuse seriously? These are some of the many questions we hope to tackle in this chapter.

Equipping Leaders, Parents, Children, and Teens

How do we prepare the church beforehand? How can we help them to be ready to deal with abuse before it happens? This work depends on having certain types of leaders, parents, childrens, and teens in the church.

Humble Leaders Who Care and Plan

To fight child abuse, start with the leadership of the church. Leaders must model a humble, teachable, and Christlike faith. They need to set an example for the church (albeit imperfectly) of what Christianity can look like (Philippians 3:17). Pastor and author Jared Wilson comments,

> A church should make humility a top requirement for leaders. Humility is observable. Look for it. And if it is hard to see in a leader, they should probably not be a leader. Everyone struggles with pride, of course, but leaders with surfacing problems of arrogance or aggression or self-centeredness will always struggle in discerning areas of power and vulnerability, which are very important to sort out in preventing abuse or handling its occurrences. You can't trust an un-humble person to sort through the fallout of abuse occurring under his watch.[1]

Arrogant, prideful, self-centered leaders are antithetical to genuine Christianity. They care more about building their own kingdoms and protecting their own reputations than caring for the abused or punishing the abuser. Selfish leaders should never be tolerated in the pulpit.

Leaders must care about protecting children. God's Word makes very clear the value of children (Genesis 1:26–28; Psalm 127; Mark 9:36–37; 10:13–16). If leadership doesn't care, you should consider finding another church.

Do the leaders of your church have a clear plan for how to deal with abuse before it happens? They should. If they place a high value on kids, and if they understand the reality of sin in this fallen world, it should be evident to them that they need to think through a plan before abuse occurs. As Proverbs notes, "The simple believe anything, but the prudent give thought to their steps" (Proverbs 14:15). Be prepared; don't simply be reactive to problems.

Vigilant Parents Who Understand

Parents need to understand the problem of abuse. Ignorance is tantamount to saying, "We don't care" or "We're too busy to think about this." Child abusers are a public hazard, and too many parents assume they are safe.

Children's and youth ministry staff can equip parents by offering classes and reading materials. The first step in helping parents is to make sure they know how to teach and instruct their children. Parents are the primary disciplers of their kids (Deuteronomy 6:4–9; Ephesians 6:1). While sex-education classes can be mandated at public schools, it is a bit more difficult to do this in a church. So, the best strategy in equipping the children about sex is to educate and encourage parents in their primary role as disciplers of their children. Help parents to understand what to say to their kids.

Church staff should help parents to understand the dreadful nature of child abuse and how to fight against it. Teach basic things like answers to the following questions: What are child abusers like? How do they operate? Which children are most vulnerable? What kind of safety skills should your children have? Who should babysit your kids—and who shouldn't? What incorrect assumptions do parents typically make about our children's safety?

By answering these questions, we are equipping our parents to understand the problem of abuse. Our goal is to create a congregation full of parents who are ready when abuse happens. They won't be ignorant or reactive or caught off-guard; they'll be prepared. This preparation will extend to the church's children, who will be educated about the problem. Appendix C of this book contains advice about what parents can say to their kids about the problem of sexual abuse.

Another step can be to help parents know how to talk to their kids about sex. In order to understand what is wrong (child abuse), children (especially the youngest of kids) need to know what is right (a healthy, God-glorifying biblical sexuality). Too many kids grow up in the church hearing the message that sex is wrong but don't understand anything about God's beautiful gift of sex to a man and woman in a covenant marriage. Why don't kids understand? Because too many parents are scared to talk about sex or be open about it at home, so kids are left to figure things out on their own.

Overall, what are pastors, church staff, and children's ministry workers expecting from parents? We are asking parents to:

- be more open with their kids about sex;
- teach a positive, redemptive picture about the beauty of sexuality in marriage and the need to stay pure until marriage;
- communicate with their children—again, in a developmentally appropriate way—what abuse is, how to prevent abuse, and what to do if someone hurts or takes advantage of them;
- teach kids not to allow anyone to touch them in areas of their body that are covered by a bathing suit;
- teach children that if they are abused they should keep telling adults until someone takes them seriously;[2]
- teach kids modesty and decorum with one another and with adults;
- teach their kids basic safety skills at home.

Many years ago several news agencies ran a series of ads that said, "It's 10 p.m.—do you know where your children are?" It was an ad campaign encouraging parents to be vigilant about their children and know their whereabouts, even late at night. Christian parents should care about "where their children are." Children are a gift and a blessing, not a burden. Christian parents recognize that they are accountable to God not only for how they feed and educate their kids, but also for how they protect and shepherd their souls. If you're a Christian parent, do you care? And if you don't care, why not? If you're struggling with these matters, contact an older, wiser Christian couple or call your pastor to talk and pray about these issues.

Children and Teenagers Who Are Educated

You should think about developing a child-safety curriculum that teaches children in a developmentally appropriate way about the following:

- what it means to stay close to home;
- who to talk to when they're lost;
- what to do when other kids pick on them;
- how to avoid strangers;
- how to not be caught in awkward situations;
- (for older kids) understanding how offenders think and act;
- what to do and who to speak to if someone abuses them.[3]

A solid children's or youth curriculum will put all of this information into a clear scriptural framework, using solid biblical instruction, and crafts or activities that equip the children. We equip kids by teaching them beforehand so they are ready at a moment's notice to face a problem, flee from an abuser, or speak up after abuse happens.

In equipping children and teenagers, we are making clear that teaching staff, children's ministry workers, pastors, and parents isn't enough. A more *thorough* strategy will include children and teenagers also. Can education of children and teens really help? In one case, a three-year-old, who was taught in church day care, later told her mother about a twelve-year-old who had molested her. The boy was prosecuted in juvenile court and later confessed to the crime.[4]

Creating a Church Culture That Takes Abuse Seriously

We've thought a lot about how to equip key people in the congregation: children's ministry staff, volunteers, church leaders, parents, children and teenagers. We've talked about *who* needs to know and *what* they need to know. Now we want to go beyond the individual roles in a church and think about the church *as a whole*. To do that, we should explain what a church culture is and why it matters.

Every congregation has a culture—a set of shared beliefs, values, and practices—that defines the church. Every pastor, member, or regular attender of your church is a culture-maker. Everything those people say or do, the things they value, the money they spend, the ways they show love to one another or work through discontentment, their hopes, their practical life choices—all of these things, plus much more, shape and define the culture in your church. What values should distinguish a church culture that takes abuse seriously?

As we mentioned earlier, *we want humble, teachable, and Christlike leaders.* If a church leader thinks of himself as being in an elite class, above the laity and in some kind of special status because of his pastoral role, then that person is capable of self-justifying, no matter how egregious the sin. Boz Tchividjian and Victor Vieth state, "Unfortunately, abusive church leaders often distort their role and authority by claiming to speak for God. This type of environment provides no accountability for those in leadership. This form of authoritarian control tends to cultivate over time and usually results in an environment where: 1) leadership is unresponsive to concerns raised by parishioners regarding suspected abuse; 2) reporting abuse to outside authorities is discouraged or even prohibited, and 3) adults are more openly valued than children."[5]

What kind of church leader takes abuse seriously? Even more to the point, what kind of church leader is not as likely to be an abuser? Christlike leaders who experience conviction for sin; who will be accountable to those around them; who will see themselves as sinners in need of a Savior (just like the rest of the church); and who will not elevate themselves above the laity but will recognize their ability to self-deceive. Church members should expect their leaders to have experienced genuine conversion to faith in Christ, to love God's Word, to see it as authoritative and necessary for their own lives (not just for their congregation), to live as examples of genuine Christian faith, and to put their hope not in this world but in the life to come. Even if we find all this, we'd further hope to have leaders who are so realistic about sin and a fallen world that they recognize they are always just a few short steps away from making a foolish decision. Thus they, more than anyone else, desperately need God's grace to not only survive but also thrive.

We want church members who are genuinely born again. If the church were full of unregenerate people, we'd expect it to look more like the world. But as the church is filled with genuinely converted people, as well as those seeking Christ, it should look different than the world. A church filled with born-again Christians *should* deal with abuse differently. They will have the same burdens and values that God has—committed to punishing the wicked (Psalm 1:4–6; 52:1–7) and upholding the weak (Isaiah 1:17; Jeremiah 7:5–7).

We want church members who are not just consumers but are committed to one another's spiritual good. America's propensity for individualism often shapes Christians to be more concerned with what they can get out of church than what they can give. Sadly, the Christian's motto is often, "It is better to receive than to give." If the members are committed to serving more than they are served (Mark 10:43–45), the church will be marked by love and self-sacrifice, not selfishness and self-reliance. Members will be invested in each other's lives and active in discipling one another. It will be much harder to be an anonymous Christian. People will seek one another out, be deliberate about building relationships with one another, and invest in the hard situations. Abusers will have a much harder time hiding in this kind of church culture where members care and are deeply invested. The abuser's hypocrisy has more of a chance of being exposed as church members are deeply invested in one another's lives.

We want a church that consistently holds out the gospel as a redemptive hope for victims. The abused want to go to a church where they can feed on the gospel weekly. Through the gospel they will see how God sent his Son to mercifully care for them. They will grow to see God's love for them and how that love can restore them to wholeness and hope. If a church genuinely believes in the gospel, then they will be quick to show mercy to victims of abuse and to take their plight seriously. If leaders and members know how to be gracious and loving to victims, it will be because they recognize what God has done for them through Christ. If the gospel is an indispensable and consistent part of the church's teaching, it will be lived out on a daily basis in the way members treat one another and especially how they care for the abused.

We want a church that is willing to hold abusers accountable. Those who relish doing evil will face God's judgment. While there is forgiveness under the cross, it would be foolish for the church to believe a quick confession without requiring an abuser to face the consequences for his or her sin. The church will be committed to holding abusers accountable for their actions.

We want a church that is willing to talk openly about sex. Sexual immorality is condemned, but the church says more than just that. The pastor preaches about the beauty of sex in marriage, as demonstrated in the book Song of Solomon. As the pastor sets the example from the pulpit, parents talk to their kids about the beauty of sex.

We want a church that is willing to talk openly about sexual abuse. Sexual abuse is not ignored. Pastors will preach against it. Children's ministry staff will train parents and volunteers. The general church culture is such that people are willing to talk openly about it. Victims receive help through individual counseling and support groups, and as they heal, the abused equip the church by telling others their stories.

We want a church where people are transparent about their problems. If the church is able to talk about sex and sexual abuse openly, it is because the church is marked out by a culture of transparency. When the pastor speaks honestly about his struggles in his Sunday morning messages, it communicates that the church is a safe place to open up about your problems. The leaders and staff encourage transparency and honesty in the Christian life. Abuse is often cloaked in secrecy and threats, so a church culture that values transparency encourages the abused to speak up and to share their struggles.

We want a church that values children. We want a church where the leaders, staff, and members place a high value on children. Children's ministry is not just day care, but an opportunity to shepherd souls. The leaders and staff have prepared policies and guidelines to safeguard kids before abuse happens. Children's ministry and youth staff and volunteers take their responsibility to care for kids seriously, including preventing and responding to abuse.

A Prayerful and Purposeful Approach to Abuse

You might look at this list and be a bit discouraged. "My church looks nothing like that!" What do you do if you feel like you are in an unhealthy church environment, dealing with church leaders and staff who don't seem to care about fighting child abuse, or if you aren't sure how to help your church deal with the problem of abuse?

Start by praying. The apostle Paul wrote: "Do not be anxious about anything, but in every situation, by prayer and petition, with thanksgiving, present your requests to God" (Philippians 4:6). Paul reminds us that everything we do—that's right, *everything*—should be done prayerfully. To pray is to acknowledge that we can't fight this problem on our own but are dependent on God to help us. So, as you equip key people in your church and think about how to build a culture that takes abuse seriously, start by praying:

Oh, Lord, we recognize that there is evil in the world.
As your Word reminds us,

> *Everyone has turned away,*
> *all have become corrupt;*
> *there is no one who does good,*
> *not even one (Psalm 53:3).*

Show mercy to the victims of abuse.
Let their hope be in you.
Heal them of their hurts and pain.
Help them to find satisfaction in your Son.
Remind them that your Son died for them, so that they might find
*   mercy, hope, comfort, and forgiveness.*

Bring your wrath against the evil doers, those who plot and deceive
*   in order to do evil.*
Show yourself to be just and right.
Punish the evil for what they have done.

Show salvation among your people, Lord.
Let them see and know your great mercy. Amen.

CHAPTER 13

. . . .

GETTING TO KNOW
THE PEOPLE AND RESOURCES
IN YOUR COMMUNITY

As a pastor, children's ministry director, or lay leader, you might face a day when you have to call Child Protective Services (CPS) to report an abusive parent in your congregation. Picture two scenarios:

Scenario #1: You make the phone call to CPS. You describe what happened, answer questions, and talk for a total of twenty minutes. Then you begin the waiting game. No one calls you back. The family doesn't hear for weeks. Finally, someone calls the family to investigate the situation. A few days later, CPS sends an investigator over to the house. All the while, no one at CPS is able to update you or give you a progress report when you call. You're in the dark and just have to wait and pray. Meanwhile, the victim and family are hurting, so you need to get them help. You talk and pray with them, but don't know how to help someone who has been abused. You're not even sure whom to call or if there is a good counselor in your community. If you are a pastor, you wish you'd paid more attention to the counseling classes when you attended seminary, but at that point you hadn't realized how much counseling you'd have to do as a pastor or staff member. You spend a few hours searching the Internet and making phone calls to try to find a decent counselor who will give the abused family members help sometime relatively soon.

Scenario #2: You pick up the phone and call a staff member at CPS, someone you have known and built a friendship with over the last few years. You describe what happened, answer questions, and talk for about an hour. The next day, the CPS staffer calls you back and tells you who will be assigned to the case. A social worker calls the family the next day and visits them the day after. She not only gets the kids into a safe house immediately but also begins to work with the police to get the abusive parent investigated. You also pick up the phone and call a very competent and reliable counselor in your neighborhood, who is able to see the family members that week. The counselor is kind, compassionate, thoughtful, and does a good job in caring for the abuse victims.

Which situation would you rather be in? In this chapter, we consider our eighth strategy: getting to know the people and the resources in your community. Do you know whom to call in your community? Do you know what professionals or organizations can come alongside the victim and your church to help you sort through abuse? Let's consider both questions in turn.

Don't Be an Arrogant Church

If abuse were to occur in your church, what kind of reaction would you *typically* expect from the leaders or the church as a whole? You'd hope the church would be humble enough to seek outside help. Yet, what you too often find is the church responding with a self-reliant, prideful, self-righteous, arrogant, or protectionist disposition.

Some churches fail to follow the law because they don't feel like they are subject to the laws of man. They often preach against worldliness and assume the world has nothing to offer the church. If abuse occurs, they think it is an internal matter and should be handled by the church. Church leaders or members look at texts like 1 Corinthians 6:1–8 (don't let Christians take legal matters into the world) or Matthew 18 (Christians should confront Christians who are in sin) and think, "We should deal with this on our own." They are not humble, teachable, or wise enough to see they need help.

Pastor Jared Wilson comments, "A church must be honest about what it can and can't do. Too many churches assume help found outside the church body is by definition 'worldly' or that all problems must be handled totally in-house. This is foolishness. A wise church will make use of legal authorities if necessary, qualified and trained biblical counseling services, consultants, etc."[1]

If Pastor Wilson is right (and I think he is), then it's worth further exploring some reason for churches to go outside its walls to ask the civil and governing authorities to help with an internal matter of abuse.

Reasons to Ask for Outside Help

Experts often comment on how churches botch up investigations or make the work of secular authorities harder because they are not competent to investigate abuse. There are four reasons why churches should not settle for in-house investigations but be humble enough to call outside authorities.[2]

First, churches usually do not have people who are trained to handle the abuse.[3] Consider what kind of professionals are needed to handle an abuse case properly: forensic interviewers who know how to draw the information out of a child graciously, without re-traumatizing him or her;[4] police with extensive experience in cross-examining abusers; and mental health professionals who know how to document the signs and symptoms of abuse in children.

Second, any delay by the church in reporting abuse can result in the loss of important evidence that can be used against the abuser.[5] Pornography, sex objects, or other items might be destroyed, or evidence on the child might be absorbed or washed away. The abuser might use the delay to pressure the child not to say anything or to recant what he or she has already said.[6]

Third, any delay in reporting child abuse to the civil authorities is likely a violation of the law.[7] In many states clergy are mandated to report suspected child abuse immediately, and in some states there is even a designated time period. Idaho, for example, requires abuse or neglect to be reported within twenty-four hours.[8]

Fourth, churches that conduct an internal investigation open themselves up to greater liability.[9] If the church does an incompetent investigation or if the abuser gets away with pressuring victims or evidence is lost, the church puts itself in a legally precarious position.

Does the Bible Justify Using Outside Help?

The reasons listed above are not explicitly from the Bible; they are all legal and pragmatic. So, Christians should ask: How do we justify getting outside help based on what we see in the Bible?[10]

In Genesis 9:5–6, we see that God establishes the power of the sword for the sake of a "reckoning" when harm comes to a human being, which means he explicitly authorizes governments to protect, among other things, the bodies and persons of children. This is the state's job, and we can thank God that he has given someone that job.

In Romans 13:1–7, Paul describes how God has established governing authorities and how churches are to submit to their laws, which would include laws about reporting child abuse. The one who does good should not fear (v. 3); it is the one who does wrong (the abuser) who should be afraid because the government is appointed to carry out God's wrath against the wrongdoer (v. 4). When pastors or church leaders keep reports of child abuse to themselves, they usurp the authority God has given to the state—an authority for which they *should* be grateful.

But some will ask, "Can't the state abuse its authority?" For example, a lot of Christians fear CPS removing children from their homes for homeschooling or for spanking. Yes, the state can abuse its authority. But keep in mind that when the state actually *does* overstep its authority by forbidding parents from doing what God has commanded them to do, then the state has begun to usurp parental authority—and, *at that point*, we should disobey it. But until this happens, we should be supporters of the state.

Biblically then, the Scriptures do encourage Christians to entrust the state with carrying out its God-given mandate to prevent and prosecute child abuse.

Don't Be a Stranger to Government Agencies

In terms of connecting with resources outside of your church, the best thing you can do before abuse happens is to build relationships *right now* with civil or governing authorities in your city or town. Consider calling and reaching out to your local police department, a local prosecutor's office, and the government agency that oversees CPS. If they are willing to give you a few minutes on the phone, introduce yourself and your church, and ask them a few basic questions, such as, "What lessons have you learned from your work that would be helpful to us?" or, "What mistakes do churches typically make in handling abuse?" Even better, if they can afford the time, take them out to lunch and ask them a host of questions related to how churches should handle abuse.

Be humble and learn from their experience. Take the time to get to know the people and build relationships with them. Afterward, send a thank-you note, acknowledging that in their busy schedule, taking time to help you was both a privilege and a kindness they were willing to afford you.

In large cities or townships, don't be surprised if you're ignored because civil or government services are often understaffed and overwhelmed with their work. Nonetheless, be persistent and gracious in your pursuit of a relationship.

Finding a Good Counselor

The second best thing you can do before abuse happens is to find a competent, godly counselor in your community who is skilled at working with abuse. If you are a pastor, you might start by calling some of the other area churches you trust and asking them if they have a referral list for counselors. Don't reinvent the wheel; other churches will probably already have gone through the trial and error of looking for a good counselor, so benefit from their wisdom.

Your *ideal* counselor is going to be someone who has a clear commitment to faith in Christ; who is careful and wise in handling God's Word; who is sensitive, compassionate, and caring to abuse victims; and who has training and experience in handling abuse cases. Short of this ideal, when you are facing an actual abuse situation in your church, you should think carefully with the leadership of the church and the victim's family about who might be a good fit. Not every counselor will be a good match for every situation.

If Abuse Strikes, Will You Be Ready?

Remember the two scenarios we presented at the start of this chapter—the poorly prepared person, who didn't know whom to call or what to do, and the well-prepared person, who was ready at a moment's notice to respond because he had done his homework in advance. Which one will you be?

Paul writes, "So whether you eat or drink or whatever you do, do it all for the glory of God" (1 Corinthians 10:31). As Christians, we want to do everything with excellence, including how we prepare for abuse—so that in the last day, we will be found faithful to the great task of shepherding and protecting our children.

Three Strategies for Responding to Abuse

CHAPTER 14

· · · ·

HELPING A CHURCH
TO BE RESPONSIBLE BY REPORTING
CHILD ABUSE

Of all the kings in the Bible, David is most famous. His many heroic deeds included conquering cities (2 Samuel 5), defeating great armies (2 Samuel 8), and even slaying the Philistine giant Goliath (1 Samuel 17). Like many kings, David's life was also full of tragedy, including his adultery with Bathsheba, the murder of her husband Uriah, and the consequent death of their newborn son (2 Samuel 11–12).

David, like us, was a sinner who made mistakes. One of his greatest is recorded in 2 Samuel 13. During this part of David's life, we find his eldest son Amnon agonizing over his love for his beautiful sister Tamar. Along with one of his advisors, Amnon cooks up a plot to deceive David and Tamar. He pretends to be ill and asks David to send Tamar to cook food and serve him. David asks his daughter to go to Amnon, and like any dutiful daughter would, she goes, prepares the bread, and bakes it, all in the eyesight of Amnon. But when she tries to serve it to him, Amnon refuses to eat it. He sends everyone away, and invites her to his bedroom so he can eat it from her hand. As she does what he asks, Amnon grabs Tamar and demands that she come to bed with him. She pleads with him to stop, "Don't force me! Such a thing should not be done in Israel!

Don't do this wicked thing. What about me? Where could I get rid of my disgrace?" (vv. 12–13). But he refuses to listen to her, and the text says, "since he was stronger than she, he raped her" (v. 14). Incest between a brother and sister was forbidden by the Levitical laws (cf. Leviticus 18:9), but what made this horrific act doubly outrageous was that Amnon threw her out after he had intercourse with her. The law also said that if a man seduced an unmarried woman, he must marry her and was not permitted to divorce her (Exodus 22:16; Deuteronomy 22:28–29). Tamar went away, grief-stricken, and her life was plagued with shame and disgrace. Her brother Absalom gave her shelter and plotted revenge against Amnon. King David got angry at Amnon (v. 21) but did nothing to address this incident.

In this story, David's silence is deafening and his inaction inexcusable. As a father David was responsible for righting Amnon's wrongs and caring for Tamar after the rape; even more so, as king, he was responsible for administering justice in the whole land of Israel.[1] And yet, David, as father and king, showed favoritism to his oldest son (2 Samuel 3:2) rather than deal with the injustice done to Tamar.[2] Some have suggested that after David's murder of Uriah and adultery with Bathsheba, he no longer had the "moral courage" and "clarity of judgment" to lead the nation of Israel, let alone his family.[3]

David's silence and inaction should be a lesson to the church. One of the worst things anyone could do upon encountering abuse is *not* to say or do anything. In the face of abuse, if a Christian does nothing, that is tantamount to being irresponsible. Responsible Christians will do something about evil when they encounter it. They won't turn their backs on it but will seek to redress it.

Up to this point in the book, we've dealt with *prevention* and *preparation*. We have been trying to answer questions like "How can a church stop abuse?" or "How can a church make sure it is ready before abuse shows up?" At this point, we make a shift to think about how to *respond* to abuse. The sad reality is that in a sinful world, far too many churches are affected by abuse. Statistics reveal the story: In 2011, an estimated three million children received some kind of

Child Protective Services (CPS) response.[4] Parents, relatives, and partners make up approximately ninety-one percent of the perpetrators who mistreat and abuse children.[5] Some experts have estimated the rate of sexual abuse among the general American population to be one in ten, but others have argued it might be as high as one in five.[6]

So, our new question is, "How should a church responsibly and wisely respond to allegations of abuse or the presence of an abuser?" Our last three chapters seek to answer this question.

In this chapter, we'll think about our ninth strategy: helping a church to be responsible by reporting child abuse. Practically speaking, that means following the laws of the land, reporting to civil and governing authorities, and allowing the authorities to do their job. Silence should never be an option in the face of such great evil done in our churches.

Why Children and Adults Don't Report Abuse

There are a variety of reasons why a child or an adult would hesitate to report abuse. Let's consider some of them.

Why Don't Children Speak Up?

When children are abused, they are put in a very vulnerable position, and their hesitancy to report shouldn't be surprising. Sometimes children will not say anything because they have been silenced by their abusers, who use threats or bribes to keep the abuse a secret. Children who are threatened and hurt by abuse will be afraid, and fear often leads to painful silence.

Other children will not say anything because they are dependent on their abusers for food, clothing, or shelter (e.g., when the abuser is one's parent). Therefore, these children don't say anything out of a fear of something worse happening. Will the alternative—foster care, removal from the home—be even worse?

Children also may not say anything out of sheer loyalty to an abuser. They don't want to betray their mother, father, uncle, aunt, or grandfather. To do so would bring shame on the family and disgrace for everyone. If an abuser is someone in a position of authority over the child, the child might mistakenly think that revealing the abuse is somehow rebellious—that he or she is not submitting to the abuser's authority.

If the child is young, she may not even understand what sex is or comprehend the wrong that the person is doing to her.

Sadly, many child abusers will corrupt the child's thinking by creating a toxic theology. They use religious language in a twisted way to justify abusive behavior and delude the child. The abuser says things like "You are preventing me from hurting others," "This is what God wants," or "This is God's will for you."

Why Don't Adults Speak Up?

Adults will not report for very different reasons, all of which are inexcusable.

Sometimes adults don't report because of pride, self-righteousness, or arrogance, thinking, "We can handle this problem on our own" or "The world has nothing to offer us."

Doubts or uncertainty slow many people down. Maybe a person sees the signs or symptoms of abuse but doesn't want to deal with it and denies or minimizes or rationalizes the problem away.

There can be a concern for harming someone's reputation. Even if the charges are false, once allegations become public, the person can be labeled for a long time as an abuser. In that vein, a person might also be concerned about the havoc this might wreak on a family—splitting them up or harming the family name. Many are slow to do something that might ruin a family.

Some will accuse the child of fabricating a story and again be concerned about ruining someone's life based on the child's "mythology." So they won't say anything.

There is also a problem among some professionals, who in encountering instances of child abuse, should report it. Many don't receive proper training about child abuse and, therefore, not surprisingly, don't follow through with reporting like they should. One study found that sixty-five percent of social workers, fifty-three percent of physicians, and fifty-eight percent of physician's assistants were not reporting all cases of suspected abuse.[7]

Whether we are dealing with children or adults, there are enormous obstacles to reporting. To head off these excuses, church leaders need to be very deliberate in their planning beforehand and in their response to abuse.

Mandatory and Permissive Reporters

What is the difference between a mandatory and permissive reporter?[8]

In hearing of, witnessing, or suspecting abuse, a *mandatory* reporter is someone who by law *must* report it to police or CPS. Mandatory reporters usually include school teachers, day care workers, police officers, doctors and nurses, licensed counselors, and, in some states, clergy.[9] No matter what kind of mandatory reporter the person might be, it is important for that person to understand whether he or she is obligated to report only in the confines of professional duties or also when volunteering at church.

What standard do we use to decide if we are going to report or not? Many might think you need to have concrete proof or at least be certain about the abuse before you report. But that sets the standard too high. Rather than waiting until you have *reasonable cause* to report, you should report as soon as there is *reasonable suspicion*.

To help define the latter term, child safety expert Beth Swagman says that a person has reasonable suspicion when "a reasonable person seeing a similar bruise or hearing a similar story would come to a similar understanding about the probable cause of the bruise or assault. Reasonable suspicion does not imply actual knowledge or certainty, as in, 'I know what happened!' Instead, reasonable suspicion suggests that reasonable people have sufficient general knowledge of appropriate and inappropriate interactions to be suspicious about a particular incident."[10]

Permissive reporters essentially include everyone who is not a mandatory reporter. A permissive reporter is someone who upon hearing of, witnessing, or suspecting abuse, is not legally mandated to report but *may* choose to do so. That said, I would argue that if a Christian has reasonable suspicion that child abuse has occurred, he or she *must* report it.

A believer has a higher moral and ethical standard than the law creates and thus is under the same obligation as a mandatory reporter to do something about the abuse. Responsibility is not just a matter of being a good citizen (i.e., doing what is helpful for society). Responsibility as a Christian primarily means doing what God asks of us, which in the case of child abuse would mean doing everything we could to protect children. In the end of time, when we stand before God and look back on our lives, we would hate to find out that children continued to be abused because we didn't do anything and to hear God's rebuke, "Why didn't you do anything about the abuse?"

There are several other reasons why a permissive reporter should report. Delays could result in the loss of physical evidence or give abusers a chance to try to cover their tracks by disposing of evidence or pressuring victims not to say anything.

Clergy Privilege and Moral Obligations

Some states allow clergy not to report if the abuse is revealed in the context of confession. This is referred to as the clergy-penitent privilege, which is a legally recognized privileged communication between the parishioner and clergy.

On this issue, Beth Swagman writes, "When clergy choose to suspend the clergy-penitent privilege in order to report suspected child abuse it's not always clear what the outcome will be. Such occasions are rare, and seldom does the accuser challenge the clergyperson's decision to report. What clouds the issue is whether the denomination represented by the clergyperson adheres to a doctrine or practice of *confessional*. The courts have typically upheld the right of clergy to hear the confession of an abuser without reporting it when the clergyperson is following a denominational doctrine of the confessional."[11]

Therefore, if the denomination has a practice of confessional, the clergy does not have to report the abuse—and according to Swagman, many do not. Only a few states have nullified the clergy-penitent privilege and require clergy to report abuse.

In some states, clergy are mandatory reporters, which should nullify this whole question of clergy-penitent privilege. But tragically, some clergy still try to invoke the privilege and end up protecting the abuser. Lawyers and child-abuse experts Victor Vieth and Boz Tchividjian comment, "If the pastor is a mandated reporter and failed to report instances of child physical or sexual abuse to the authorities, this conduct is criminal in many states."[12]

Some denominations that adhere to the practice of confessional press the clergy not necessarily to report abuse but to encourage the abuser to confess his or her sin to the authorities.[13] They hope to protect the integrity of the confessional by allowing the pastor or priest to keep a parishioner's confidences while at the same time getting the sin out in the open. Is this a fruitless strategy, considering how rarely abusers would be willing to take responsibility for abuse and face the consequences for their sins?

I want to argue that as every Christian has a moral and ethical responsibility to report child abuse, so then clergy have an even greater obligation to do so. They are charged with the responsibility of being shepherds of God's flock (1 Peter 5:2). The Chief Shepherd, Jesus Christ, has entrusted them with responsibility for the sheep, and so the pastor or priest must give up his life for the sheep (John 10:11), just as Jesus has done. He must take this charge seriously because one day he will give an account for how he cared for these souls. If a child is hurt, neglected, or abused, the pastor has a responsibility to protect that sheep from the wolves who threaten his precious life (John 10:12).

What does this mean for clergy? If a pastor or priest witnesses, hears about, or suspects abuse, he is morally obligated to report. Protecting an abuser is not acceptable. The first priority should never be protecting the confessing abuser, or prioritizing a vow of confidentiality during confessional, but protecting children.[14] Anything short of that will be an affront to God and contrary to how the Scriptures teach shepherds to care for their sheep. It is in the best interest of both the abuser and the children that the secret be told and the weakest and most feeble sheep—our children— be protected.

A Few More Things about Reporting

When a child reveals abuse to an adult, the adult should listen carefully and ask open-ended questions. Care should be taken not to suggest answers. Don't rush the child through the conversation. Be patient and don't be scared of his or her emotions. Because this is a very sensitive subject, there will probably be crying as the pain and shame is brought out of the darkness and into the light (2 Samuel 13:18–19; Ephesians 5:7–13).

After the conversation with the child, the adult should document the details of the conversation. Don't write things out *during* the conversation; instead, focus on the child as he or she talks to you. A write-up should include identifying information about the victim and alleged perpetrator; any details from the conversation, including the nature and frequency of the abuse; the date the report was written; bruises or injuries that are visible on the child; and any emotions displayed in the conversation. Don't ever ask the child to undress to show other bruises or markings. Later on, as the adult tries to remember the conversation, if he is at all uncertain about the details, he should not go back and re-interview the child. Let the child's next conversation be with a trained professional.

If the abuse occurs in the context of the church, the person who has reasonable suspicion of abuse usually needs to talk with both church officials and civil authorities; although it is possible for a church to be so corrupt that the person would just need to go to the police or CPS.

Every church should have a designated contact person—someone who is ready to receive and respond to allegations of abuse. Where there is a contact person, anyone with knowledge or reasonable suspicions of abuse should immediately reach out to this person and talk through the relevant information.

If the person talked with the church's designated contact person, it should not be presumed that it is now the church's responsibility to report the abuse. A responsible Christian who witnesses, suspects, or hears of abuse should also promptly report it to civil and governing authorities. Churches often try to conduct their own investigations in order to decipher the legitimacy of the abuse claims, but as we stated earlier, initially this is not the role of the church. Church investigations too often make things worse, not better.

If a child or teenager has shared with you allegations of abuse, don't let your doubts, fears, or concerns slow you down. A helpful phrase to remember is this: *Resolve doubts in favor of reporting.*[15] Even if church members or the leadership of the church disagree with the need to report, a responsible Christian who has reasonable suspicion about abuse will report to police and CPS.

Police are responsible for investigating allegations of abuse and then turning them over to a prosecutor, who decides if there is enough evidence to bring a charge against an alleged abuser. CPS is responsible for the well-being of the child, not the prosecution of the abuser. CPS's main concern is to make sure the child is safe, and, if not, to place them in a context where the abuse cannot be continued.

You should call CPS (or whatever agency is charged with the welfare of children in your area) in any of the following cases:

- the child is related to the abuser or lives with the abuser;
- the child is being abused by a nonrelative at home;

- the child's safety is at risk and the parents are not protecting the child.

Engage a local police department in the following cases:
- the child does not know the abuser;
- the child is not related to the abuser and does not live with the abuser;
- the child may have contact with a nonrelative abuser without protection;
- the child is under the authority of a nonrelative abuser at a location other than the home.[16]

If a person who witnesses, suspects, or hears of abuse is unwilling to make a report, and if church leaders or staff believe there is reasonable suspicion that abuse has occurred, someone from the church needs to contact the police and CPS. Not only is there a moral obligation for the church to act to protect children from any further harm, but the church might also later bear legal liability if it knew about the abuse but did not do anything about it.

If a person is not sure if he or she has reasonable suspicion and grounds to report, it is good to talk over the situation with legal counsel or discuss the case anonymously with the police or CPS. Ask to speak with someone who handles allegations of abuse and regardless of the outcome of the conversation, be sure to document the conversation and the name of the person you spoke with.

It is possible to file a report anonymously, but if a person chooses to do so, he or she should do it in the presence of a third party. That way, if the person is later charged with negligence in reporting, there will be a witness to testify to the fact that the person was not negligent but in fact responsible to report allegations of abuse in a timely fashion. In addition, if someone files an anonymous report *on behalf of* a witness, anonymity may not extend to the witness but only to the reporter. However, one should avoid this situation if at all possible, as it will inevitably result in delays in the investigation and prosecution of an alleged abuser and potentially keep the child in a dangerous situation.[17]

It is important to understand that there are criminal penalties for failing to report. Failure to report can result in a fine or jail time. Protection is afforded from legal and civil litigation if the report is made in good faith.

Beth Swagman distinguishes between a false report, where a child or an adult lies about abuse, and an unsubstantiated report, where an inquiry is made by police or CPS and they are unable to conclude if abuse has occurred. In the latter case there might be some evidence but not enough to prosecute. Importantly, she notes, "The incidence of unsubstantiated complaints is far greater than the number of false reports."[18]

If the authorities decide not to do anything, the church may still need to investigate, especially if there is a possibility of the alleged abuser continuing to harm children. For example, suppose a missionary returns from overseas and there are allegations of abuse stemming from his or her work in a foreign country. The police will not investigate because the abuse does not fall under their jurisdiction, but the church should act based on its knowledge of the allegations. A church can choose to conduct an internal investigation and hire an outside expert to do an investigation. Conducting an internal investigation could prevent the church and denomination from future liability.[19]

If the authorities decide that they are not going to pursue a report, it is also advisable for the church to keep written reports or a log of the allegations; to document any reports made to the police or CPS; and, if the children are in the congregation, to do their best to continue a relationship with the children. If signs or symptoms of abuse increase in frequency, the church will need to make a report again to police and CPS.[20]

Is Someone Lying to Me?

You might wonder, "Is the child lying to me about the abuse?" In life in general, children sometimes do lie. After all, they are sinners just like you and me. But with accusations of abuse, Beth Swagman states "children or youth are more likely to lie to *protect* a parent-abuser out of love for that person" rather than fabricate a story about abuse.[21] It is less likely that a child is lying about abuse and more likely that he or she is taking a courageous step and asking for help. Any time a child shares about abuse, we should take the allegations very seriously.

In regard to abuse, it is not unusual for people to suspect the child of lying and, in contrast, take adults at their word. But keep in mind that some adults will lie, too. A spouse or a relative is more likely to accuse the child of making up a story than to own up to a family member who is abusing children. Tragically, some children will tell a parent about abuse by a relative or other parent, and the response will be to warn that child not to say anything or to shame him or her for sexual behavior.

If there is someone to suspect of lying, let it be the offender. Swagman reminds us, "The reality is that offenders lie, too. They have much to lose by admitting they've hurt a child—including their job, their family, their reputation in the community, and their family's image. And the greatest loss could be the offender's personal freedom if he or she is prosecuted and imprisoned. No one has more to gain by lying and thus convincing others not to report their suspicions."[22]

An abuser's goal is probably to cloud the whole situation in secrecy and silence so that he or she can continue abusing. When allegations of abuse surface, don't be quick to suspect that a child is fabricating a story. It is possible that some adults are lying in order to stop abuse from being brought out into the light.

Creating and Implementing Reporting Policy

This brings us back to the importance of having a child protection policy (CPP) that provides clear guidelines on how, what, and when a church should report to civil and governing authorities. A lack of clear guidelines leaves the church in a position of inconsistently responding when abuse occurs. It's better to think things out in advance and have a clear line of protocol to follow.

A CPP's section on reporting should include the following:

- Guidelines for mandatory and permissive reporters.
- Instructions on reporting to the church's designated contact person for individuals who witness, hear about, or suspect abuse. Just because a person talks with a church staff member does not mean it relieves him of his responsibility to report to police or CPS. You can't make assumptions about what the church will do nor think, "Now it is their responsibility to deal with it!" Child-safety experts Cobble, Hammer, and Klipowicz warn, "Don't assume that requiring such a person to report suspected abuse to a designated church official will discharge their reporting duty under state law."[23]
- An outline of *whom* the church will contact and *what* the church will do in response to abuse. A clear process needs to be outlined for the church leadership and staff to follow. For example, after reporting to police and CPS, will the church contact medical personnel, their lawyer, or their insurance provider? Will the perpetrator be immediately removed from the programs with children? Or will the church bar this alleged perpetrator from services or the church property? Will the congregation and parents be told? If the alleged perpetrator is staff, will it result in suspension or termination of his or her job? How will the church care for the victims? What about church discipline?

Along with policy, it is important to train the congregation, making sure they understand the following:

- The importance of reporting abuse.
- The typical obstacles to reporting.
- Definitions of child abuse, sexual abuse, and physical abuse.
- Description of signs and symptoms of child abuse. Church workers should be trained to distinguish appropriate and inappropriate adult behavior toward children, especially in regard to physical contact.
- What to do if a child confesses abuse and what kind of documentation is necessary to make a report.
- Whom to talk with at the church if a person hears about, suspects, or witnesses abuse.

In regard to training volunteers and staff about reporting, several experts note, "The church does not want to create an atmosphere of fear or suspicion. Proper training can help workers see how reporting can be done honestly and discretely without generating undue suspicion or anxiety."[24]

The End of the Matter for King David

The sad result of David's silence and inaction is that matters in his family got worse. Absalom, Tamar's older brother, sought revenge for Tamar's rape by killing his brother Amnon (2 Samuel 13). Absalom immediately fled in order to avoid punishment, but he eventually came back and overthrew his father's throne, took over his kingdom, and slept with his father's concubines (2 Samuel 15:1–12; 16:15–22). David had to flee Jerusalem with his most trusted friends to preserve his own life (2 Samuel 15:13–19:8).

Much like David, if the church fails to be responsible by reporting, things will go from bad to worse. So, do the responsible thing as a Christian, and resolve doubts in favor of reporting. The integrity of the church and the lives of precious children hang in the balance.

CHAPTER 15

HELPING A CHURCH TO RESPOND WISELY TO VICTIMS, THE CONGREGATION, AND THE MEDIA

How can churches wisely respond to child abuse? Consider the story of Vienna Presbyterian Church and the aftermath of an abuse scandal involving their former student ministries director, Eric.[1] From 2001 to 2005, Eric was the youth minister for the church's growing youth group. The church was thrilled as he did a great job at mentoring and connecting with the youth. But public appearances can be deceiving. At the very same time, under a cloud of secrecy, Eric had initiated intimate relationships with girls in the youth group, getting involved romantically, professing his love and desire to get married—and as each got older, initiating sexual contact. One girl tried to come forward but was ignored; for several others, the church's response made it difficult to report what had happened. Eric, on the other hand, when news broke about the allegations, received encouragement from many church members, including support during the trial, help moving out of his condominium, and financial gifts from members. Some church folks even blamed the girls outright, implying it was their fault. They claimed it would be hard for a young man to resist temptations from young women.

In 2008, pastor David Jordan-Haas joined the church staff. Even though it had been several years, he recognized the wrong that had been done and sought to rectify the situation. The church formed an abuse outreach ministry in 2009 and soon afterward heard for the first time the full story of one of the women who had been led astray by the former student ministries director.

This process culminated with the church going public about the situation, taking ownership for the wrong done, and apologizing to the victims. On March 27, 2011, senior pastor Peter James preached a sermon on sexual abuse to the congregation at Vienna Presbyterian Church. Turning to a group of young women who had been abused by Eric, Pastor James stated, "We failed as leaders to extend the compassion and mercy that you needed. Some of you felt uncared for, neglected, and even blamed for this abuse. I am sorry. The church is sorry."[2]

Legality and Liability Setting the Course?

This might seem like a great story of redemption as an earthly institution (in this case, a church) takes steps to rectify wrong done in its midst. But if you read widely in accounts of churches responding to abuse, you'll find that the response of Vienna Presbyterian Church is very unusual.

Lawyers and insurance companies often balk at the idea of taking ownership for wrongs done in a church. As lawyers, insurance companies, and churches sort through how to deal with abuse, what arises are the competing demands of Scripture on the one hand—where repentant sinners admit mistakes, accept responsibility, and apologize—and a litigious society on the other hand—which warns against self-incrimination and encourages doing everything one can to defend against potential lawsuits.

If a church owns its mistakes and apologizes, it risks legal challenges, increased liability, and possible financial ruin. Vienna

Presbyterian Church took the bold move of going public, but not everyone was happy about their decision. As expected, some in the congregation were upset. Unexpectedly, their insurance provider gave them significant pushback as well. On March 23, 2011, a lawyer hired by the company, GuideOne Insurance, sent a warning to church officials, "Do not make any statements, orally, in writing or in any manner, to acknowledge, admit to or apologize for anything that may be evidence of or interpreted as (a suggestion that) the actions of Vienna Presbyterian Church . . . caused or contributed to any damages arising from the intentional acts/abuse/misconduct by the youth director."[3]

But in a letter sent to congregants the very next day, the church's governing board took a different course. The letter stated, "Members of Staff and of Session are profoundly sorry that VPC's response after the abuse was discovered was not always helpful to those entrusted to our care."[4] In a sermon on March 27, Pastor James took things one step further, asserting, "We won't hide behind lawyers. . . . Jesus said the truth will set us free."[5]

Most churches don't follow the example of Vienna Presbyterian. Most churches let legal and liability restrictions dictate how they will respond to abuse cases. Kelly Clark, a lawyer who has sued many churches over the issue of child abuse, states, "Believe it or not, I have never gotten an unequivocal apology for any of my clients from the Archdiocese of Portland (or from any Archdiocese for that matter), from the Latter-Day Saints Church, from the Seventh Day Adventist Church, or from the Boy Scouts of America. Oh, they will agree to letters of regret, they will agree to letters acknowledging the victim's pain and suffering, or the wrongness of the abuse. But I have not yet been able to get an institutional official to say: 'As a representative of this institution, I apologize profoundly to you for what our man did to you. It was wrong, he betrayed you and betrayed your trust. And because he represented us, we betrayed you and violated your trust. I apologize and am so sorry.' Why is that so difficult?" [6]

The Christian tenets of openness and truthfulness create greater liability in a judicial world. So says Jack McCalmon, whose company often helps insurers by showing churches how to set up abuse prevention programs. What church insurers want most is to limit liability. McCalmon explains, "The insurance company has a contract with the church that says, 'If we're going to put our assets on the line, we want you to perform in a way that protects our assets and interests.'"[7]

This puts churches in a defensive posture. The priority is given to protecting oneself rather than rectifying the wrongs done within a church. As Pastor Jordan-Haas would say in the wake of the abuse scandal, "We really seek to change, institutionally and relationally, and that comes at a cost."[8] Most churches are unwilling to risk the costs as they face the very real possibility of incurring legal damages they couldn't afford to pay, bankruptcy, and the demise of the church.

What then is a proper response for a church? Should legal and liability restrictions set the agenda for a church's response? If not, what should? This brings us to our tenth strategy: helping a church to respond wisely to abuse. What does wisdom look like as a church deals with the aftermath of abuse? We want to think carefully about how the church should lovingly care for the victims, communicate with the congregation, and deal with the media.

Caring for the Victim and the Family

No matter how much work is involved in sorting through an abusive situation, the church needs to be continually mindful of caring for the victim. As soon as the allegations are revealed and the authorities contacted, care for the child or teenager needs to begin immediately. Don't let victims and their families struggle with the ongoing effects of abuse on their own.

Abuse can have a host of aftereffects on the victims. Victims can act controlling in relationships because they need to feel safe. Others might feel powerless to deal with life because they couldn't stop abuse. Perceptions of body image and identity will be distorted. Victims may talk about themselves in derogatory terms, saying things like "I am worthless," or "I am trash." There can be self-destructive acting out with drugs, sex, alcohol, food, or spending as the victims try to find ways to self-soothe or escape the pain. Self-injury, even mutilation or suicidal ideation, can also be a struggle.

The victims' understanding of God's will and their relationship with God will probably also be severely skewed. When a person who was supposed to protect you betrays you, it makes it very difficult to accept God's love and grace. God will likely be seen as punitive and judgmental rather than accepting or loving. Relationships can be very unstable, with a consistent push-and-pull—sometimes wanting intimacy, other times feeling scared to be close. Trusting others, especially those in authority, is often difficult. It is not uncharacteristic for victims to have a series of very short relationships, not really letting anyone into their life with any depth but continuing to move from relationship to relationship. Therefore, it is your duty as a church to provide whatever spiritual, medical, and emotional support is necessary to bring healing and redemption to these situations.[9]

Churches can often be at a loss in how to help, especially if they have not encountered abuse before. Over the long term, victims need to feel the church's support in many ways; but in the short term, the best thing that a pastor, staff, or members can do is simply to listen.[10] The wounds of abuse are deep, so it will take lots of love to deal honestly with the harm done by the abuser. Let the victims tell their stories and be patient with them as the healing process can often take a long time.[11]

Apply the gospel very liberally to this child's or teenager's life. When he or she acts out as a result of the abuse, do not apply a regimented law, but give the gospel generously.[12] So says Victor Vieth: "The gospel may be the only tonic the abused child has *never* experienced."[13] Help the victim to see that Christ empathizes with his or her sorrow because he too was stripped and beaten. He suffered and was hated. Remind him or her of Christ's love for children (Mark 10:13–16) and his warnings for those who do harm to children (Matthew 18:6).

In addition to patiently listening and applying the gospel liberally, there are a variety of other things the pastor, members or church staff can do to help. Even if the child or teenager goes to a counselor, one concrete way fellow Christians can help the victim is to untangle the distorted ways that abusers use religious language to confuse children and teenagers. Abusers often use a distorted theology in order to justify their actions.

Pastors, staff, and church members should also be careful and thoughtful in how they speak to victims. They should not give the child or teenager religious platitudes or a quick, superficial application of Scripture.[14] At some point, in speaking to victims, they should make a clear moral declaration that the abuse was wrong and also encourage the victim that speaking up was scary but the right thing to do.

Pastors, staff, and members should remind the victims of the need for forgiveness. Forgiveness is important, especially because it can free an abused child or teenager from bitterness or anger. But be careful: some Christians will recklessly press on victims the need for forgiveness. Forgiveness can't be forced. It has to come from a heart rooted in the gospel and ready to forgive as a response to what God has done for us in Christ.

The pastor and church members should also regularly pray for the victim, offer practical assistance, like providing meals, and stay in frequent contact.

The church also needs to be mindful of the victim's family. One of the most overlooked parts of the healing process is the church's need to shepherd the parents and the siblings, not just the victims.

In an age of fast food and quick fixes, leaders or fellow church members might wonder why counseling and dealing with these issues takes so long. The church needs to recognize that in dealing with the trauma of abuse, healing will take time. No one can rush the process. The pastor and church need to be committed to care for the victim for the long haul.

Victims' Advocates and Counselors

Two roles that are important in facilitating the church's care for victims are a church advocate and a counselor. Both can help the church in doing a better job in caring for victims.

Churches should consider appointing an advocate in order to not lose sight of the victim's needs. Initially, after the allegations of abuse emerge, there will be a lot of turmoil, conversations, and meetings in an effort to deal with the abuse. But six months or a year later, silence or lack of interest by the church can tempt the victim into thinking that he or she has been forgotten. To head this problem off, it is wise for church leaders to designate an advocate—someone in the church to keep tabs on the victim and be in the front lines of caring.[15] This person can help harness the resources of the church to show support throughout the process. For example, this person can arrange rides to doctor's appointments. He can arrange for meals or childcare for siblings when the parents need to be at important events, like court dates. He can pray regularly and check in regularly, giving the victim and family a consistent sense that the church has not forgotten them and still cares. He or she can also serve as a liaison between the victim and the church's leaders, advocating for the needs of the victim and keeping the leadership updated.

Counselors can also be very helpful in caring for victims. The church's leaders and the advocate can help by recruiting a competent counselor. At the outset, the church leaders or the advocate or the victim's family should ask the potential counselor questions about how much experience he or she has in treating abuse. In picking a counselor, Vieth has warned, "An incompetent counselor may be worse than no counselor at all."[16]

Prioritizing the Needs of Victims

Having considered what the church, advocates, or counselors can do to care for victims, we should also consider what the victims want from this process. The sad irony of this is that most victims *don't* want a lawsuit and large monetary settlements but feel compelled to pursue legal battles because churches ignore them, minimize the abuse, or even fight against them. Most victims are more interested in hearing an apology, seeing the abuser brought to justice, and witnessing genuine church reform that helps prevent other children from being hurt. Lawyer and child-abuse expert Kelly Clark, who has prosecuted dozens of Christian institutions on the issue of child abuse, has said that nonmonetary responses by a church—such as an apology from the leaders, symbolic gestures like a garden dedicated to abuse survivors, and a face-to-face dialogue with church leaders—all can bring a tremendous amount of healing to victims.[17]

The temptation is to prioritize the needs of the church over the needs of the victims. If the church takes a defensive posture of protecting itself against possible lawsuits or increased liability, often engagement with the victims will be a low priority, or in many cases nonexistent. Care for the victim should be the highest priority.

Clark also argues that it is possible for the church to do the *smart thing* of protecting itself and also the *right thing* in caring for the needs of the victims.[18] In fact, if the church takes care of the needs of the victim first, what "they will find is that it goes better for them after that." Clark states that if churches care for the needs of victims first, "it takes all the venom out of the situation…. [The victim] no longer has a need or basis to vilify" the church.[19]

Communicating with the Church

Another important area to consider is how church leaders and staff will communicate information about the abuse to the congregation.

The decision of *when* to communicate with the congregation can often be tied to restrictions put on the different parties involved, especially by legal counsel. The appropriate time for communicating to parents or the congregation can vary, from after the initial complaint all the way to the completion of the investigation, and wisdom is needed to discern the best timing.[20] There are two wrong ways to approach this issue of communication: either saying nothing to the church, which later on will be especially troubling to parents, or telling the church everything in explicit detail.[21] Neither approach is appropriate.

The legal concern is the possibility of a lawsuit over defamation or invasion of privacy. The idea of "qualified privilege" is instructive here. Child-safety experts Cobble, Hammer, and Klipowicz explain that church leaders may talk with the congregation about a specific child abuse situation because of a "qualified privilege" that protects "communications made in good faith on any subject matter in which the person communicating has an interest, or in reference to which he has a duty if such communication is made to a person having a corresponding interest or duty."[22] In other words, the church leaders can communicate with the congregation about the abuse because those members have a relevant interest in the matter, especially when it comes to the care and protection of their own children.

If the church leader communicating with the church knows what he is saying is false or shares the information recklessly without any regard to truth or falsity, then the leader and the church are liable for defamation and invasion of privacy. The key to this "qualified privilege" is to communicate only with members because they are the people who have a direct interest in knowing about it. To that end, there are two ways to communicate about a specific abuse case with the congregation.

First, church leaders can send a letter directly to the members of the congregation. The letter should fall under the parameters of qualified privilege if it is sent only to members, marked as confidential, and limited to explaining only the facts of the situation.

Second, the leaders can discuss the matter in a members' meeting. The same parameters would apply: members only and the leaders sharing only the facts of the situation, not speculation or personal opinion. If you're involved in carrying out this communication with your church, don't identify the victim unless he or she asks to be identified. Help the church to understand what happened, but only tell the church what is necessary. Help them to understand that the leaders have responded immediately, the victim is safe and is getting help, and the authorities are investigating the alleged perpetrator. Encourage other victims to come forward if they have been abused by this person or anyone else.

Because gossip is a frequent problem with Christians (Proverbs 11:13; 20:19), church leaders and staff need to be careful to maintain appropriate confidentiality. If the information is shared with the membership, the members should also be warned about confidentiality. Everything should be handled with great care and consideration toward the victim, the accused, and their families. Moreover, any means employed by the church to communicate with its members should be reviewed beforehand by the church's legal counsel.

Talking with the Media

In dealing with media, the best way to avoid false rumors or distorted facts is to come up with a strategy for media relations.[23] For example, one element of a possible strategy is to make a statement to the media. A statement lets the community know that the church not only knows about the abuse but is doing something about it. The statement can also be especially helpful to the victim and family. As Swagman states, "For the victim and victim's family . . . it provides an open and honest acknowledgment that their story was believed."[24]

Another element of this strategy is to designate someone from the church to speak on its behalf. This spokesperson should be a member of the church and should take great care in what is expressed. He or she should not speculate but simply stick to the facts of what is known and adopt a humble and gracious tone with the press. Defensiveness, anger, or blame can be misinterpreted, so the spokesperson should avoid all three and focus on how the church is dealing with the abuse and especially the care of the victims.[25] The person should be humble enough to say, "I don't have an answer to that," or, "I've been advised not to address that," rather than making up answers or saying, "No comment." One pastor, who dealt with the media in the aftermath of abuse in his church, states, "It is unrealistic to think you can take a 'no comment' stance with the media. Newspeople will find someone else to interview if an official spokesperson doesn't deal with them."[26] The spokesperson will help the media and the community understand that the church takes the allegations of abuse seriously.

The End of the Matter for Vienna Presbyterian Church

To this day, Vienna Presbyterian has yet to be sued. One can only wonder if there is a larger lesson to be learned here. If a church has the courage to care for the victims rather than protect itself, will it really go better for both parties in the end?

Yes, it will. As Christians, our faith in God is demonstrated when we don't solely follow a path of self-protection but instead show that as a church we want to do the right thing by caring for victims. Plan now for those hard moments by resolving to fight for the downtrodden. Prove through your actions that you don't want any of God's children to suffer through the long-term effects of abuse by themselves.

CHAPTER 16

HELPING A CHURCH TO DEAL WISELY WITH A CHILD ABUSER

Imagine if a sexual offender showed up at your church. Maybe you discovered he is a sexual offender through a criminal background check, or he might have volunteered the information to someone at the church. Regardless, what do you do with him? A thousand questions abound: *Do you let him come to church, or should you keep him off the property? How do you protect the kids if he is in the building? Should you permanently bar him from children's ministry? Should you bar him from any involvement in the church's ministries, even if kids are not involved? What if the offense happened years ago when he was a kid or a teenager?*

Our final strategy deals with how a church can deal wisely with a child abuser. The reality is that the church has a responsibility to the abuser as well as the abused, and it needs to think through how to handle both parties.

The Accused

If a church volunteer or staff member is accused of sexual abuse, the church should immediately have the person removed from any contact with children or teenagers. Too many organizations have gotten in trouble because they allowed the accused to stay in contact with children even after allegations were revealed. Better to remove the alleged offender if you are suspicious of a problem than to potentially expose more children to abuse. As the accused is removed from contact with children, the church should also report the suspected abuse to civil authorities, follow through with any other guidelines of the child protection policy (CPP), care for the victims, and communicate with the congregation as needed.

Many offenders have learned that if they cry and express remorse, the church will be quick to forgive, with little or no consequences for previous actions. They are looking for cheap grace.[1] Too many pastors are liberal with the gospel of grace but slow to apply the law and consequences. Why? Because many pastors feel compelled to forgive if a sinner is remorseful, and they feel like they have not legitimately forgiven if they have to hold the penitent person to the consequences of past sin.

If the accused is a believer and not a religious hypocrite looking for cheap grace, what should we expect from him or her? Genuine sorrow will lead to repentance—a true turning away from the sin and toward God in faith (2 Corinthians 7:9–13). This involves a willingness to make right what one has done wrong (Luke 19:8) and a willingness to own earthly consequences for sin (Luke 23:41). If most child abusers in church settings are well-practiced liars and pretend to be religious, they will say what they need to say in order to avoid consequences for their actions and to continue to have access to children. So, a legitimate way to test if the abuser's repentance is genuine is to see if he is willing to prioritize the care of the victims, report himself to police, plead guilty in court (rather than make the victim go through the trauma of a court trial), and commit himself to a child-abuser treatment program.[2] Pastor Jared Wilson comments,

> On that note, we must educate our church what grace is, what repentance is, what forgiveness is, and what reconciliation is. What do they look like? We must understand that the gospel is

often a severe mercy to abusers, even genuinely repentant ones, and so it means consequences — disciplinary in the church, legal outside—and accountability. Too often "grace" for the abuser adds more abuse to his or her victim. But justice can be grace. It is amazing how often churches fail in this regard, pushing for relationships between victims and their abusers, spiritualizing some kind of reconnection as if it honors God when really it is a cheapening of grace and often just a way to sweep events under the church rug. In the kingdom of God, the helpless, the hurting, the trampled on, the *abused* take precedence. Any truly repentant abuser would agree to that. We must remember that a victim's safety and healing is vastly more important than a church's convenience.[3]

In dealing with the accused, the church should not settle for cheap grace. Cheap grace is not genuine Christianity. Real grace doesn't preclude real consequences (Galatians 6:7–8). It is a myth to think that true forgiveness by the victim and the church means that the offender should never face consequences for sin.[4] Hold the child abuser accountable for his sin; hold him responsible to do everything he can to right the wrong he has done. To do so is genuinely to love the abuser as well as the victim.[5]

The Visitor

What if someone handed you a note that said, "A visitor named Mr. Jones just walked in and is seated in the balcony. He's a known sex offender." Would your church be ready at a moment's notice? What if the convicted child abuser came back to church several weeks in a row?

There are four things that a church should do if a known abuser shows up at the church:

First, *the church should be prepared to have a member shadow the offender at all times when he or she is on the church premises.* The escort should ensure that the offender does not engage with any children or teenagers or visit the children's ministry or youth classes at the church. If the offender returns to church, he or she should be contacted and alerted that he or she is not allowed to be at the church without a chaperone. Based on the history and the nature of the past abuse, the church might need to consider establishing a separate service for him at the offender's home or at another location with a select number of members from the church. This allows the church to prioritize the protection of children and also find a way to meet the spiritual needs of the offender.[6]

Second, *someone on staff should contact the offender's parole officer and the local prosecutor's office to find out the specific terms of his or her probation.*[7] It is important to understand the terms of the offender's probation so the church can abide by the law. For example, if the offender is not allowed in public settings with children, the church should contact the offender and make clear to him or her that the church will not violate the law.

Third, *someone should review court documents or other records to verify the offender's past offenses.*[8] It would not be unusual for the child abuser to lie or cover up aspects of past offenses. The church should verify from other sources what really happened.

And fourth, *if the offender continues to attend, the parents in the church should be informed.* The parents should be told so they can decide what level of supervision is appropriate in protecting their children.

None of this should be done ad hoc; these steps should be carefully traced out in the church's CPP.

The Convert

We must allow for the possibility that some offenders *have* become genuinely saved. But how can we tell whether someone is a Christian or is just playing a role in order to once again obtain access to children?

Genuine believers will repent of their sin (Mark 1:15; Acts 3:19), trust in Christ (John 3:16; Romans 3:21–26), and evidence the fruit of conversion in their life (Luke 6:43–45). The difficulty comes in analyzing a known child abuser. The child abuser builds his or her life on a lie. In order to gain access to children, the abuser puts on a double life in order to convince the community that he or she is a trustworthy character. If the person is an alleged or known offender, one can't help but wonder if this person is once again faking religion in order to fool the church.

Or is this person genuinely seeing the work of the Holy Spirit in his life as a true convert? There's no easy way to answer these questions because it is incredibly hard to discern if a predator is truly converted or not. No one wants to be fooled a second time. On the other hand, we don't want to hold a genuine child of God away from the fellowship he or she needs to grow in Christ.

Suppose the church leaders decide that the offender is a genuine believer. What then? If the abuser is genuinely saved, he has the Holy Spirit in him (Romans 8:9–10). He can grow in Christ (Philippians 2:12–13), and it is possible for things to change in his life (Philippians 1:6). Paul writes in Galatians 6, "A man reaps what he sows. Whoever sows to please their flesh, from the flesh will reap destruction; whoever sows to please the Spirit, from the Spirit will reap eternal life" (vv. 7–8). Paul reminds his readers of a sowing and reaping principle—the consequences of an offender's abuses must be dealt with, even if those abuses occurred before his conversion. In other words, if the offender is genuinely converted, it will evidence itself in a willingness to accept the consequences for sin, report to police, seek treatment, and make reparations for sin—much like Zacchaeus, who after his encounter with Christ recognized the magnitude of the wrongs he had done and desired to do whatever he could to right those wrongs (Luke 19:8).

If the church does allow the offender to come to services, the leadership must ensure that proper precautions will be taken for the sake of the kids. Even if the offender is a believer, and even if the offense occurred before he became a Christian, he or she should be permanently barred from children's ministry. We don't put alcoholics in bars after they are recovered because we know the power of temptation and how quickly they can fall off the wagon. Offenders have developed a deviant desire for children. We don't want to provoke that desire again by putting them around children. Evil desires, when acted upon, always lead to sin and death (James 1:15).

The church must affirm that sexual offenders can become born-again Christians—that they can face a deep conviction of sin and genuinely want to turn from their former lives. Even so, the church should also assume that many child abusers are so deeply entrenched in their sinful habits that there is *not* a genuine desire to change. Too many offenders are just out to take advantage of religious people, so don't be fooled by their words or actions.

The Member

What if the sexual offender eventually asks to join the church? How should the church deal with him or her? Assuming that the above recommendations were carried out while the offender was visiting the church, a couple more steps should be taken.

Have the offender agree to and sign a code of conduct. These conduct guidelines should require that the offender do the following: agree to a thorough background check; verify and detail all past abuses; allow the church leaders to disclose this information to the congregation; refrain from any communication or activities with children or teens, both inside and outside of the church; and be accompanied by a chaperone whenever the offender is at church. Church staff should warn the offender that any violation of these terms could result in church discipline and a barring from the church. The child abuser's consent to these items should be in writing.

Have the child abuser agree to the church's prioritizing the needs of the abused. If the offender is genuinely repentant of his or her sin (2

Corinthians 7:9–11), it should be evidenced in his or her willingness to defer to the needs of the victims. For example, if the victim does not feel safe in the same building with the offender, the offender should be willing to find a different church. This would allow the victim to remain behind and feel safer in his or her church. If the offender does not willingly defer the needs of the abused, he shows that he does not understand the gravity of his own sin.

Clergy or Other Staff

We've recounted numerous times the very sad reality that clergy or youth ministers will prey on children. When clergy or church staff abuse—really, when anyone offends in the name of God—it is a "triple wrong."[9] Not only are we dealing with the abuse itself and the betrayal of trust but also with the manipulation of Christianity as a justification for the abuse.

If any church staff member admits to or is convicted of abusing children, there should be a zero-tolerance policy. He or she should be permanently removed from ministry.[10] Catholic leaders had to learn this lesson the hard way through thousands of lawsuits, and they have now made clear that zero tolerance is the best way to handle child abuse.[11] Their words will be tested by their practice in the days ahead. L. Martin Nussbaum and Theresa Sidebotham argue, "Enforcing zero tolerance is difficult for many pastors because when a perpetrator appears sincerely remorseful, zero tolerance seems heartless and, worse, contrary to a gospel of redemption. In church situations, ministry leaders need to consider the children at risk and to distinguish between redemption and job restoration."[12] Likewise, Pope John Paul II told the cardinals of the United States, "There is no place in the priesthood or religious life for those who would harm the young."[13]

What Should the Church Do?

Churches face the deeply complex and challenging responsibility of loving the abused and the abuser. The church's response to an offender depends on whether the offender is a confessor who wants cheap grace, a visitor, a genuine convert, a potential member, or church staff.

Some offenders should be asked to find another church to protect the victim. Others should be welcomed as members under strict precautions. Others should be permanently barred from church staff. All should have their repentance "tested" to see if they are genuine. Knowing how to respond, in any of these situations, requires wisdom from God.

CONCLUSION

· · · ·

OUR WITNESS, OUR RESPONSIBILITY, OUR FEARS, AND OUR HOPE

If, God forbid, someone did get abused in your church, what would the people in your community say? "That's the church where that little boy got abused." Or maybe even, "Did you hear about the abuse case in that church? Those Christians are a bunch of hypocrites." This is not the witness that churches want to leave in their communities.

What are you hoping for? You want to have a powerful gospel witness, where your neighbors hear about the love of Christ and see it lived out among them. That's how you want to be remembered, right? Protecting the children under your care is a way to preserve your gospel witness in your community. If you are careful and work hard to reduce the risk, God in his infinite kindness might let you preserve a gospel-preaching, Christ-honoring witness in your community. You don't want to be remembered as the church where offenders got away with abuse.

Our ethical and moral responsibility as Christians is to protect the children whom God has entrusted to us. According to the Bible, children are a heritage and a reward from God (Psalm 127). Whoever dares to harm them should heed Jesus's warning: "If anyone causes one of these little ones—those who believe in me—to stumble, it would be better for them if a large millstone were hung around their neck and they were thrown into the sea" (Mark 9:42).

Lord willing, you are now better equipped to understand this problem and begin to take some active steps to prevent abuse. Reading this book was your first step. What's next? Pray, talk with leaders in your church, find ways to assist the staff, and start implementing a child protection policy in your church. Your children and teenagers are well worth the time and effort.

If you're walking away feeling more concerned that a child abuser might harm your children, that's probably a good thing. The realities of child abuse are deeply disturbing, and they should motivate us to take seriously the protection of children in our churches.

However, far be it from me to end this on a note of fear. As Christians, where does our hope finally come from? Not in anything we can do in this world but in the God of grace who equips us to walk in his wisdom and strength. As followers of Christ we must not live in fear but trust God. We should serve our children and our churches with the same confidence King David wrote about as he faced trials and difficulties:

When I am afraid, I put my trust in you.
  In God, whose word I praise—
in God I trust and am not afraid.
  What can mere mortals do to me? (Psalm 56:3–4).

Appendices

APPENDIX A

. . . .

A REALLY QUICK GUIDE TO WRITING AND IMPLEMENTING A CHILD PROTECTION POLICY

In her book *Preventing Child Abuse: Creating a Safe Place*, Beth Swagman offers this helpful counsel about child protection policies (CPPs):

> No single policy works well everywhere! The child safety policy that works well in one church or nonprofit organization will not necessarily work well in another church or organization. Sample policies may help [you] visualize what the final product will look like, but an organization that adopts another organization's document without first examining how well it fits its own setting will often find that it should have tried it on before buying it.[1]

Rather than giving you sample policies, I thought that a better way to serve you would be to identify the important *parts* of a CPP and offer a strategy for *implementing* your new policy. I won't build the engine for you, but I can help you get started.

What Are the Important Parts of a CPP?

Let's start by tracing out the vital elements of a CPP and why they are important. This is not a comprehensive list but is meant to give you a sense of some of the things that might be included in your own CPP.

The Vision and Mission of Children's Ministry. The vision tells you where you want to go; the mission tells you how you are going to get there. What are the priorities, values, and goals for your children's ministry, and how do you want to realize them?

For example, our vision for children's ministry at Capitol Hill Baptist Church (CHBC) is "Generations of Godliness." In the end, when Christ returns, we want to be known as a church that raised up many generations of faithful believers to continue on with the great faith we have been given by our fathers and mothers in the faith (Deuteronomy 6:4–9; 2 Timothy 3:14–15).

Our mission states, "The children's ministry of CHBC exists to glorify God by . . .

- Maintaining a safe and secure environment;
- Supporting and encouraging parents who are primarily responsible for teaching biblical truths to their children (Ephesians 6:4);
- Making the whole counsel of Scripture known to children, with special emphasis on the gospel (Deuteronomy 6:6–9; Romans 1:16–17);
- Praying for the children and relying on the Holy Spirit to regenerate their hearts through the faithful teaching of his Word (Romans 10:17; Ephesians 2:4–10);
- Living faithfully before the children and modeling for them how Christians are called to respond to God, interact with each other, and interact with the world around us (Matthew 5:16; 1 Corinthians 11:1);
- Encouraging children to learn to serve and to not just be served (Mark 10:43–45);

- Maintaining the highest ethical standards such that volunteers and teachers always live and serve above reproach, protecting the reputation of the gospel of Jesus Christ;
- Preparing children to one day walk with God as adults—which means getting them ready to be a part of the public services and, Lord willing, one day, become fully participating adult members."

Parameters for the Policy. It is important to define the parameters in which the policy does or does not apply. Defining the scope of the policy limits liability by helping to make clear what falls inside or outside the responsibility of the children's ministry staff or volunteers.

Personnel Summary. This section outlines who will participate in children's ministry and what their roles and responsibilities are. For example (again, taken from our own CPP),

> "*Staff* are the paid employees of the church. All full-time church staff are required to receive a background check regardless of whether or not they have direct contact with children.
>
> *Volunteers* are those who work with children and are not in the employment of the church. All volunteers who serve in children's ministry are required to go through *both* the children's ministry training and screening procedures before they serve. Volunteers include childcare workers, team leaders, hall monitors, teachers, and anyone else who serves the children. The term 'volunteer' will be used throughout this policy manual as an all-encompassing term for anyone who serves the children and is not church staff."

Other personnel terms you might consider using (and defining) are *adult, minor, helper, deacon, pastor,* and any term designating a governing body of the church.

Expectations of All Staff and Volunteers. As the personnel summary gives specific responsibilities for each role, this expectation section is more general. What expectations do you have for everyone who serves? For example, a policy might say, "All children's ministry staff and volunteers share a responsibility for loving the children as Christ loves them and for setting an example of proper Christian conduct in the way we live our lives."

Training and Screening Procedures. What training classes or screening procedures will the church employ? Be sure to list them all in this section. Some questions you might need to answer here include the following: How long should a person be a part of the church before he or she is allowed to serve with children? What is the minimum age of a volunteer? What kind of training do volunteers need to complete? Is there an application, and is the volunteer required to fill it out? Will the church do background checks, reference checks, social media checks, or any other form of investigation into the person's past, such as interviews or fingerprinting? Who approves the volunteers? Will there be repeat checks in the future, and, if so, how often will they occur? Is the staff required to undergo screening procedures?

Expectations for Classroom Settings. This includes the two-adult rule, adult-to-child ratios, and guidelines for visibility, discipline, physical touch, and food and drinks.

The Two-Adult Rule. Because child abusers like to hurt children in isolated settings, experts recommend having two adults around at all times. To take it one step further, because family members are often unwilling to report wrongdoing by relatives, experts also recommend that two *unrelated* adults serve together. Also, this section of the CPP should specify gender requirements (e.g., When two adults serve together, must at least one of them always be a woman?).

Adult-to-Child Ratios. What kind of ratios should you maintain to keep your kids safe? If you are not sure of this, call a local day care center or school to find out what ratios they use.

Visibility. When classes or programs are in session, what degree of visibility is required? Do doors need to be open?

Discipline. When a child misbehaves, how should the staff, childcare workers, or teachers handle it? Trace out what are appropriate forms of correction and even the process of correction. Explain what a staff or volunteer is prohibited from doing. Be clear about what the volunteer should do if children are out of control, likely to harm other children or themselves, or unresponsive to acceptable means of discipline.

Physical Touch. What is appropriate and inappropriate touch? Spell it out. Be sure to define this for *adult-to-child, teen-to-child*, and *child-to-child* relationships.

Food and Drinks. What foods or refreshment are allowed and not allowed in the children's ministry areas? Will volunteers feed the youngest children, or are parents required to do this? Will the older kids get snacks and drinks? If so, what will they be served? How will allergies be handled?

Protective Rules and Safety Guidelines. This section should address other things we need to do to keep our kids safe.

Sickness and Wellness. What should staff and volunteers do to prevent communicable diseases? What should volunteers do when they change diapers, wipe noses, or handle blood spills? When should a child not participate in a classroom? What will the staff look for when they screen for sick children? How will toys and equipment be cleaned? This section should also include a description of universal precautions, like using latex gloves when changing diapers or washing hands before or after contact with bodily fluids or disinfecting toys after use.

Check-in and Checkout Process. What does a parent need to do to sign in and sign out a child? What system is in place to accomplish this, and how do parents and volunteers use it? What happens if a parent loses the designated form of identification (wristband, sticker, etc.)?

Restroom Procedures. Who is allowed to take children to the restroom? Just as the two-adult rule is applied to the classrooms, is there some version of this rule that can be applied to taking children to the restroom? Or instead of the two-adult rule, can a single adult take children to the restroom, but you require at least two children to go with that adult to the restroom? At what age is a child allowed to use the restroom on his or her own?

Transportation Guidelines. Who is allowed to drive the children? How many adults and children or teens must be present to transport children or youth? What kind of consent is required by parents? Should the driver keep a log of trips? How often will a driver's driving record be reviewed? What state or federal requirements for car-seat, seat-belt, or airbag safety should be stated in the policy? What exclusions should be made for relatives who are transporting children or teenagers?

Off-site or Out-of-Town Event Guidelines. Be sure in this section to state restrictions, such as limits on physical contact and a prohibition of leaders being alone with children or teens, leaders dating teenagers, private communication between leaders and children or teens apart from parental supervision, and alcohol or illegal drug use. The following questions should also be considered: What is the minimum age difference between a volunteer or staff member and children or teens? What is the minimum number of staff, volunteers, children, or teens required for an event or program? What should staff or volunteers do if a child's behavior warrants removal from an off-site or out-of-town event? What kind of safety guidelines should the staff and volunteers adhere to when off-site? What kind of written consent is needed from parents? What kind of sleeping arrangements should the kids have? Are children allowed to leave the site and, if so, under what conditions? What kind of guidelines do you need for bathroom use during off-site or out-of-town events? What kind of guidelines do you need for discipline during off-site or out-of-town events? What should volunteers or staff do in response to bullying?

Emergency Response Plan and Evacuation Procedures. How does the church plan to deal with an evacuation? A tornado or earthquake? A live threat like a shooting or some other security hazard? A missing child or a kidnapping?

Prevention Plan for Child Neglect and Abuse. This section should start by defining important terms such as *neglect, abuse,* etc., and then proceed to describe what steps the church is taking to prevent abuse.

Reporting and Response Plan for Child Neglect and Abuse. This section will address the following: Who is the church contact person in handling abuse allegations? What are the guidelines for mandatory or permissive reporters? What are the state guidelines for reporting? What will the church do in response to allegations? Will it report to police or CPS, remove the alleged perpetrator from children's programs, notify the congregation, make sure the alleged perpetrator has a chaperone while at church, suspend or fire a staff member? What will the church do if it learns of allegations from the police or CPS? What kind of response will the church have if an adult alleges abuse when he or she was a child at the church? What are the parameters for confidentiality? How will the church handle the media?

Guidelines for How the Church Handles Sexual Offenders Who Regularly Attend or Join the Church. What will the church do if an offender attends the church one or two times or comes regularly? What if an offender wants to join the church? What guidelines and prohibitions must an offender agree to if he or she wants to join the church?

A Duty-to-Warn Policy. If an adult abuses a child at church, what obligation does the church have to inform other churches, organizations, or schools in which this adult is involved? What guidelines should the church follow in regard to warning others about abuse or an abuser, either current or past?

In your policy's appendix, you might also consider including the following:

- Signs and symptoms of abuse;
- Samples of all children's ministry forms (incident report, medical consent, transportation consent);
- Screening application (or any other type of application); and
- State guidelines for mandatory and permissive reporters.

A Strategy for Writing and Implementing a New CPP

If you're considering writing a CPP for the first time or revising your existing CPP, be sure to think through the steps listed below.[2] Keep in mind that in most churches you will probably have people who will resist your writing and implementation of a new policy. Pray and be patient as you work through this process.

Find someone in leadership who will listen to you. To start with, it will be necessary to find someone in leadership who sees preventing and responding to child abuse as an important issue. At first, your conversations with church leaders need to deal with the concept of child abuse, the legal and moral obligations of protecting children, false assumptions, and possible fears or concerns. You'll have to deal with questions like the following: Can abuse really happen at our church? Will a new policy be cumbersome and discourage people from serving in children's ministry? What are the legalities that need to be considered? What would help the church to be prepared and reduce the risk of abuse?

Equip and educate the staff, volunteers, and congregation. The next step is to raise awareness throughout the church about issues of child abuse. Ignorance of the issue is one of the chief reasons why abusers are so successful in church contexts. The church might consider a variety of means of communicating, including special seminars, Sunday sermons, bulletin inserts, articles in the church newsletter, etc. Along with educating and equipping, you are also trying to build consensus on the importance of this issue.

Write (or rewrite) your policies. After the concept of a CPP is officially approved, someone has to do the hard work of actually writing the document. Obtain sample copies of policies from other churches, but remember that your policy needs to be tailored to fit the specific needs of your church. Some churches like to form a committee that hammers out the details, but I've found that to be very cumbersome and time-consuming. It's much more efficient to designate a lead writer and then have different members of the congregation (e.g., teachers, doctors, nurses, parents, etc.) give feedback after the initial draft is finished. The last two steps of this process should be to consult with a lawyer to review the new policies and then make sure the church leadership signs off on them.

Train church staff and volunteers. Then evaluate. With a new policy in place, the church needs to be trained so that everyone is familiar with the new guidelines. Current staff and volunteers need to be re-educated, and new people need to be trained as they begin serving for the first time. After the policy has been executed for some time, it should be evaluated by staff or other church leaders.

APPENDIX B

• • • •

CHILD-ON-CHILD SEXUAL ABUSE

In the 2011 report on Child Maltreatment by the US Department of Health and Human Services, child-on-child abusers made up less than six percent of all perpetrators reported to the government, the majority of which were teenagers between the ages of fourteen to nineteen.[1] Though the percentage is low, all abuse is wrong and damaging, and the sad reality that kids abuse kids is something the church must factor in as it forms a plan for prevention and response. Here are a few important things to consider.

Distinguish between common sexual behaviors and problematic behaviors.[2] In thinking about preschool or elementary children (ages two to twelve), researchers have created a continuum to differentiate between common and infrequent behaviors, or between typical sexual play and problematic sexual behavior. Common sexual behaviors that parents report observing in children include the following:

Ages two to six:
- Do not have a strong sense of modesty and enjoys own nudity;
- Curious about differences between boys and girls;
- Curious about sexual and genital parts;
- Touch their private parts;

- Might exhibit sexual play, like playing "doctor," with siblings or friends;
- Experience pleasure when touching genitals.

Ages seven to twelve:
- Sexual play with children they know (playing "doctor");
- Interested in sexual content in media (TV, movies, radio);
- Touch own genitals at home, in private;
- Look at nude pictures;
- Interested in the opposite sex;
- Shy about undressing.

We can contrast this with behaviors that parents report are infrequent or highly unusual:
- Puts mouth on sex parts;
- Puts objects in rectum or vagina;
- Masturbates with objects;
- Touches others' sex parts after being told not to;
- Touches adults' sex parts;
- Asks to engage in sex;
- Imitates intercourse;
- Undresses other people;
- Asks to watch sexually explicit television;
- Makes sexual sounds.

Typical sexual play . . .
- is exploratory and spontaneous;
- occurs intermittently and by mutual agreement;
- occurs with children of similar age, size, or developmental level, such as siblings, cousins, or peers;
- is not associated with high levels of fear, anger, or anxiety;
- decreases when told by caregivers to stop; and
- can be controlled by increased supervision.

Problematic sexual behavior . . .

- is frequent, repeated behavior, such as compulsive masturbation;
- occurs between children who do not know each other well;
- occurs with high frequency and interferes with normal childhood activities;
- is between children of different ages, sizes, and development level, like an eleven-year-old boy playing "doctor" with a three-year-old girl;
- is aggressive, forced, or coerced;
- does not decrease after the child is told to stop the behavior; and
- causes harm to the child or others.

Use these categories to help distinguish between an incident that is problematic (and requires reporting) or something that is more typical for a child (but may still need addressing with the child and/or parents).

There is a big difference between a four-year-old playing doctor with a three-year-old and a fourteen-year-old boy getting sexual favors from six-year-old girls. The following are some questions that can be asked by church leaders or staff: Was one child an aggressor? Has there been a pattern of related behavior in his or her life? Was he curious and "playing," or was it more than that? Discernment is required to know what to do. Some situations will require barring a child from children's ministry. If the behavior is frequent, repeated, harmful, aggressive, forced, or between children of very different ages, the church leaders and staff should bar the child from children or youth activities and get help from a counselor who has experience working with children or youth.

Make sure the child protection policies define who is allowed to help. If children or teenagers are allowed to be in classes to assist teachers and watch over other children, make sure there are careful guidelines about who can or cannot help. Create a screening process for children or teens who will help in younger children's classes. Don't let them help unless you know the families and the children well; otherwise, you invite lots of potential problems. For example, an older boy who serves as the assistant teacher should not be taking a younger child to the restroom by himself. This situation isolates a child with a child, and as we mentioned earlier, the church should shape policies to avoid isolation.[3] In youth ministry, it is not uncommon to have something akin to a "five-year" rule, since college students are close in age to teenagers and the temptation to cross interpersonal or physical boundaries can be quite high.[4]

Ask about child-on-child abuse in your children's ministry application. Be sure to screen for this problem. Ask a question on your screening application like, "As a child or teenager, did you ever have sexual interaction with a child?" This question will evoke responses from abusers and victims, so staff should be ready to shepherd both categories of individuals who honestly answer this question.

How Do I Talk to My Kids about Sexual Abuse?

In the wake of the 2011 sex scandals at Penn State University, I've had a number of parents ask me, "How do I talk to my kids about sexual abuse?" While a lot could be said, I have suggested eight principles for parents to consider.

Teach Your Kids about a Healthy Biblical Sexuality

Most of us grew up in churches hearing warnings about the dangers of sexual promiscuity. "Sex before marriage is wrong!" "Don't indulge yourself or else it might go too far!" "Wait until you get married!" It's true: the Bible does condemn selfish, immoral sexual behavior. However, it also speaks of sex as God's beautiful gift to married couples.

Think about what you teach your children about sex. Do you tell them (whether explicitly or implicitly) that sex is taboo and never to be talked about? Or do they see sex as a precious gift from God that needs to be honored as such?

This also begs the question: Do you ever talk about sex with your kids? I don't mean in a crude or rude way or just in a one-time "birds and bees" conversation when hormones start exploding. What about speaking openly with your kids about sex in a dignified and God-honoring way? If you never talk about sex with your kids, that says something to them—perhaps, "We are uncomfortable talking about sex, and you need to figure it out on your own."

Parents, teach your kids about sex. Help them to see the beauty of sex. Explain to them the kindness of God in giving such a wonderfully expressive way for a man and woman to find unity in marriage. Point them to the wonderful fruit that comes from sex in the gift of children. Help them to see the glories of a healthy, God-honoring, biblical sexuality.

Be wise in how you talk to them. Kids at different ages need to hear developmentally appropriate information. A conversation with our three-year-old will be much more basic: "A man and a woman get close to one another and make babies." A conversation with our nine-year-old will be more sophisticated and will involve body parts: "The sperm goes from the man's penis into the woman's vagina, and if one of his sperm merges with one of her eggs, a new life is formed." Sounds a little bit frank, right? Maybe so, but they need to know. And if you don't tell them about sex, the world will.

If you are not really sure what a developmentally appropriate conversation looks like, you can use the book series *God's Design for Sex* by Stan and Brenna Jones. There are four age-appropriate books in this series (ages three to five, five to eight, eight to eleven, and eleven to fourteen) that help you address the topic of sex with your children.

Your goal as a parent is to teach your children what God has to say about sex. Don't let the culture define the way your kids think. They won't ever recognize the world's perspective on sex as being *bad* if you don't teach them what is *good* first.

Teach Them Modesty

Teach your children to be modest. Show your children what it means to have discretion with their private parts. There are simple things you can say to your kids, like, *Close the bathroom door. Don't be naked outside your bedroom. Don't let your siblings see you getting ready. Knock on Mommy and Daddy's door before you come in.* Teach them these things to help them preserve the dignity of their nakedness (Genesis 3:10; 2 Chronicles 28:15).

The world wants your kids to be crude, rude, promiscuous, and immodest. Look at the music videos, Hollywood movies, and fantasy novels that surround our children. But that's not all. Take a look around on Sunday mornings at church. Look at how many of the men and women (even the *Christians*) are dressed. It's not just the world but also the church that needs to think about modesty.

One simple way to be proactive and to head off child abusers is to tell your kids that no one—*absolutely no one*—is allowed to see or touch their private parts except parents or a doctor. One easy way to help your kids remember this is tell them that no one can see or touch the parts of their body covered by a bathing suit. Make this clear to your kids at an early age. Then occasionally reinforce the same message with them.

Proper Decorum and Boundaries with Kids and Adults

Every family needs to have a basic set of rules for the kids. It's important, especially for the younger children, to follow these guidelines for their own protection. *Play outside in a place where a parent can see you. Don't go into a friend or neighbor's home unless you ask your parents first. Don't stay out past dark. Answer your cell phone when we call.*

Teach your kids that they do not have to accept hugs and should not allow inappropriate contact from anyone, even other kids. Telling your kids to be cautious around strangers is rather obvious to you. But what's harder to understand is how (and why) you should protect your kids from other kids.

The reality is that children do take advantage of other children. Some children are curious and want to try things out, and they do so by experimenting on another kid. Some kids are deliberately malicious. They've seen sex in the movies. They've heard other kids talk about it. So they take advantage of another child or even force two younger children to have sex with one another. Kids who have been abused will sometimes act out by abusing younger children.

Not *all* children are innocent, naive, and sweet. A three-year-old kid hugging another three-year-old is innocent enough; an eleven-year-old boy hugging all of the little girls on the playground probably is not. Sadly, many abusers start their patterns of deviant behavior as teenagers hurting younger children. So, don't be naive as parents.

Teach your children that they have the right to say *yes* or *no* when it comes to touch and their own bodies, and show them through your actions as adults that you take their consent (or lack thereof) seriously. For instance, don't make your children hug family members or friends, but allow them to decide if they want to do so. They can instead offer a handshake or high five to be polite. Or if you're tickling them and they ask you to stop, do so and reinforce to them that people who care about them will respect their physical boundaries. Tell them that if *anyone* makes them uncomfortable or hurts them, they should tell you and that they will never be in trouble for telling you.[1]

Give Your Kids a Realistic Perspective on the World

For some Christian parents, there is a temptation to isolate their kids in a protective emotional bubble. They don't want to expose their children unnecessarily to the corruptness of this world until they are ready. Other Christian parents are much more permissive, letting their kids explore or watch things with very little concern for a filter. If you're a parent, wherever you fall on the spectrum, it's important to acknowledge that in a sinful world, bad things are going to happen to children. Some kids get sick, others die in tragic accidents, and many will be abused by adults, teenagers, or other children. At some point, we have to decide how and when to equip them for the foolishness, immorality, and brokenness of a sinful world.

The Bible's perspective on the world is very realistic. It doesn't avoid the hard things but takes them head-on. Parents often skip the hard parts because they're not sure what to say or how to explain things to their children. What do I say about the murder of Abel (Genesis 4)? How do I explain to my kids that Noah, the ark, and the floods of Genesis is not a *cute* story about animals in an ark but a *sobering* story about God's judgment of humankind (Genesis 6–9)? What should I say about David's murder of Uriah and his affair with Bathsheba (2 Samuel 10–11) or the stoning of Stephen (Acts 7)? You need to talk to your children in a developmentally appropriate way. You need wisdom about *what* to say, *when* to say it, and *how* to integrate the gospel into your instruction. But at some point and in some way, you need to choose to teach your kids a realistic perspective on sin and a fallen world. Consider how to use your Bible, with all its hard parts, as a tool to help you do that. Avoiding conversations about evil in this world, or simply letting your kids figure it out on their own, should not be an option.

Equip Your Kids to Recognize and Fight Against Abuse

Once you've given your kids a realistic perspective on a fallen world, speak specifically to them about abuse. Tell even the youngest of children something like, "There are bad people who might want to hurt you." Teach them to say *no* and to come to a parent for help.

If you have taught them what sex is, you can go one step further by teaching them what abuse is. *Remember what sex is? It's only for a husband and a wife, and it is a gift to them from God. Sex is only for two adults who are married. Abuse is when someone tries to play with your private parts or tries to force you to have sex. That's wrong because sex is only for married adults, and no one should ever play with your private parts or force you to have sex.* Again, the conversation is very frank, but that's necessary in order to help your kids understand abuse.

You might use 2 Samuel 13, the rape of Tamar by her brother Ammon, as an example of sexual abuse. This story could dispel the myth that only strangers bring harm. You can help your kids to see that sometimes even children's family members or relatives, whom they know and love, might harm them.

Also, help your children to distinguish between inappropriate touch—kissing or fondling of private areas, shoving, hair pulling, shaking, slapping, biting, hitting, slaps on the behind—and appropriate touch—a hug, a pat on the back, high-fives, or handshakes. Be as specific as you can so your kids have a clear sense of what is good or bad touch.

Teach Safety Skills

As my wife and I were walking into a shopping center with another family from our church, the mother leaned over to her children and asked, "If you get lost, what do you do and what do you say?" Her children repeated their parent's names, their cell phone numbers, and their home address, all from memory. I was impressed. The mother had taught her children how to get help if they got lost in a large shopping mall.

Take some time to teach your children what to do or say in order to be safe. What do you do if you get hurt? Do you know how to call for help on your parent's cell phone? What do you do if a kid on the playground picks on you? What if a stranger asks you to go with him or her or to get into his or her car? What happens if you get lost? What if someone tries to touch you in your private parts? As a parent, what would you want your kids to do in each of these situations?

Don't wait until something goes wrong before you say something to your kids. Get out ahead of the potential problems; be proactive and teach your kids basic safety skills before they find themselves in difficult situations. One simple way to do this is to role-play with your kids. After dinner, ask your kids to act out what they should do or say in each of the above situations. With younger children, you can be creative by using puppets to act out a harmful situation. For example, what if a stranger in the park starts playing with them, or even worse, touches them? What if someone they don't know invites them for a car ride or tries to grab them? What should your kids do? With children of any age, you can describe a difficult scenario, assign roles, and let the child or children act out what they would do in the situation. The key is to instruct them on how to respond. It's your job as a parent to equip them before they come face to face with a dilemma.

No Secrets

Children are born naive to matters related to sex. While they are young, most kids don't know what sex is or why people do it. Many Christian children are so sheltered from the world that they rarely encounter any teaching, conversations, or ideas related to sex. So if these kids are abused, they don't have categories for what is happening to them nor the moral parameters to know that it is wrong. Educate your kids to know the purpose of sex—that it is for a husband and wife, and not for anyone else.

Child abusers want to teach your kids to keep their deviant behavior secret. They will tell your son or daughter, "Don't tell your parents. Let's just make this something special between the two of us, okay?" On this point, be explicit with your children. Tell them, "Don't ever keep secrets from us. If someone teaches you to do that, it is wrong." The best way to head off an abuser is to say something to your kids *before* an abuser tries to convince them to hide something from you.

Be Invested in Your Kids

Be an ever-present reality in your kids' lives. Go to your kids' baseball and soccer games, attend piano recitals, and be present at every birthday party. Parents' absence—in some cases, very frequent absence—makes their children especially vulnerable to sexual offenders. The best way to show child abusers that you are not going to let your kids be vulnerable is to be a constant presence in your kids' lives.

Parents, build a strong relationship with your kids. Get to know them. Be a part of their world. Love them such that they will trust you more than anyone else.

APPENDIX D

. . . .

AN EXAMPLE OF A SCREENING APPLICATION

Application for Ministry to [CHURCH NAME]

Thank you for your interest in serving the children and families of [CHURCH NAME]. Upon approval of your application, the Children's Ministry Director will work with you to find a spot on our children's ministry team that will be a good fit for you based on our needs and your interests and experience.

**Please put your completed application
in a sealed envelope and place it
in the children's ministry mailbox in the church office.**

_____

Personal Information

Name: _____ Date: _____

Street Address: _____

City: _____ State: _____ ZIP: _____

Daytime Phone: _____ Evening Phone: _____

Email Address: _____

I prefer to receive information regarding children's ministry via:
☐ email ☐ phone

Family Information

I am: ☐ Single ☐ Married ☐ Divorced ☐ Widowed

Do you have any children? ☐ Yes (How many: _____) ☐ No

Membership Information

How long have you been a member of [CHURCH NAME]?

Date joined: _____

Please list any other ministries and activities you have participated in at [CHURCH NAME].

Prior Experience

Have you taught or cared for children in any church or parachurch ministry before?
    ☐ Yes (Please describe, including dates and places).
    ☐ No

Please describe any training, education, or other factors (including musical training) that would apply to your ministry to children.

Training

I attended Childcare Training on _____ (date)

Personal Commitment

In dependence on the Holy Spirit and by God's grace,
    ☐ I will be faithful and dependable in this ministry.
    ☐ I will seek to learn more about ministering to children as information and training are available.
    ☐ I will faithfully pray for the children who are under my care.
    ☐ I commit myself to continuing personal spiritual growth.
    ☐ I commit to knowing when I am scheduled to serve and arriving to serve on time.
    ☐ I have read, understood, and commit to abide by the policies contained in the Children's Ministry Handbook.

Signature: _____

Date: _____

Personal References

Every applicant for participation in children's ministry must provide two personal references. The Children's Ministry Director will contact these references.

The applicant waives the right to view reference statements.

If you have been a member of [CHURCH NAME] for *less than one year*, please list the following:

1. A pastor or church leader from the church you most recently attended;
2. A person with whom you have worked or served in the past who knows you well. (If you have served in children's ministry in the past, please list someone who served with you in that context.)

If you have been a member of [CHURCH NAME] for *more than one year*, please list the following:

1. A pastor, small group leader, or other church leader who knows you well;
2. Another member of [CHURCH NAME] who knows you well and can attest to your suitability to work with children.

Name: _____

Address: _____

Phone: _____

Email: _____

Relationship: _____

Name: _____

Address: _____

Phone: _____

Email: _____

Relationship: _____

Verification of Information

The information contained in this application is true and correct to the best of my knowledge. I authorize [CHURCH NAME] to contact any references or organizations listed in this application. Furthermore, I authorize such references and organizations to provide [CHURCH NAME] with any information they may have regarding my character and fitness for working with children. I release [CHURCH NAME], its agents, and all such references and organizations from any and all liability for any damage that may result from furnishing such evaluations to you, and I waive any right that I may have to inspect references provided on my behalf.

I further state that I have carefully read the foregoing release and know and understand the contents thereof. I sign this release as my own free act. This is a legally binding agreement that I have read and understand.

Signature: _____

Date: _____

Consent for a Criminal History Background Check

[CHURCH NAME] has contracted the services of [SCREENING COMPANY NAME] to perform criminal background checks on all children's ministry applicants. A national criminal records search is performed. The following information is required.

Name: First _____ Last _____

Middle _____

Address: _____

_____

Date of Birth: _____ Social Security Number: _____

Driver's License Number/State:_____

Reports are confidential and viewed only by [CHURCH NAME] [STAFF MEMBER'S NAME OR TITLE] and filed in the applicant's secured file.

Personal information is protected under the Privacy Act.
Reports obtained from [SCREENING COMPANY NAME]
will be guarded accordingly.

Note: Any reported misdemeanor or felony will be discussed with you and [STAFF MEMBER'S NAME OR TITLE] and may be grounds for denial of application to work with children.

Name: _____

Confidential Information

The following questions are designed to help us promote a safe, secure, and loving environment for the children who participate in our programs. This information will be kept confidential, viewed only by [STAFF MEMBER'S NAME OR TITLE].

If you would like to discuss any of these matters further with [STAFF MEMBER'S NAME OR TITLE], please simply indicate that below or leave the form blank.

Answering "yes" to any of these questions will not necessarily disqualify you from participating in children's ministry at [CHURCH NAME].

1. Have you ever been a victim of abuse?

(Many people have experienced abuse at the hands of others. Most victims of abuse abhor such behavior and are especially alert and sensitive to the need to provide a safe and caring environment for children. At the same time, residual effects may remain in some people's lives, including a hesitancy to report suspected child abuse, which is why we ask this question.)

☐ Yes
☐ No
☐ I would like to discuss this.
Comments:

2. Have you ever been accused of, participated in, pled guilty to, or been convicted of child abuse, child neglect, or any other crime against a minor?

☐ Yes
☐ No
☐ I would like to discuss this.
Comments:

3. Have you ever been convicted of or pled guilty to a crime (other than minor traffic violations)?

☐ Yes

☐ No

☐ I would like to discuss this.

Comments:

4. Have you deliberately and repeatedly viewed pornography in the past three years? *(This includes reading, watching, listening to, or in any other way using pornographic material, including books, magazines, television shows, movies, the Internet, or telephone services.)*

☐ Yes

☐ No

☐ I would like to discuss this.

Comments:

5. Do you have any ongoing sin struggles that you think would keep you from ministry to children?

☐ Yes

☐ No

☐ I would like to discuss this.

Comments:

6. Do you have any communicable diseases or infections such as tuberculosis, Hepatitis B, HIV/AIDS, MRSA *(Methicillin-Resistant Staphylococcus aureus)*, **etc.?**

☐ Yes

☐ No

☐ I would like to discuss this.

Comments:

7. As a child or teenager, did you ever have sexual interaction or contact with a child?
   ☐ Yes
   ☐ No
   ☐ I would like to discuss this.
   Comments:

APPENDIX E

. . . .

CHILD ABUSE AND NEGLECT
TRAINING SHEET[1]

How is Child Abuse Defined?

Child abuse or neglect is any recent act or failure to act resulting in imminent risk or serious harm, death, serious physical or emotional harm, sexual abuse, or exploitation of a child (usually a person under the age of eighteen, but a younger age may be specified by CPS in cases not involving sexual abuse) by a parent or caretaker who is responsible for the child's welfare.

Sexual abuse is defined as follows:
- Employment, use, persuasion, inducement, enticement, or coercion of any child to engage in, or assist any other person to engage in, any sexually explicit conduct or any simulation of such conduct for the purpose of producing visual depiction of such conduct; or
- Rape, and in cases of caretaker or inter-familial relationships, statutory rape, molestation, prostitution, or other form of sexual exploitation of children, or incest with children.

There are many signs of child abuse. Any one sign may not mean anything, but if there are a number of signs, or if they occur frequently, you may suspect maltreatment. Signs can be physical, emotional, or sexual, as in the following examples.

Physical

- Unusual bruises, welts, burns, fractures, or bite marks
- Frequent injuries, always explained as accidental
- Wearing concealing clothing to hide injuries
- Seeming frightened
- Seeking affection from any adult
- Being unpleasant, hard to get along with, demanding, frequently disobedient

Emotional

- Being apathetic, depressed, withdrawn, passive
- Seeming overly anxious when faced with new situations or people
- Being disorganized
- Being distrustful
- Being rigidly compulsive
- Taking on adult or parental roles and responsibilities
- Throwing tantrums or seeming impulsive, defiant, antisocial, aggressive, self-destructive
- Being fearful or hyper-alert, showing a lack of creativity and exploration

Sexual

- Having torn, stained, or bloody underclothing
- Experiencing pain or itching in genital areas
- Having an STD or venereal disease
- Appearing withdrawn or engaging in fantasy or baby-like behavior
- Having a poor relationship with other children
- Being unwilling to participate with other children

- Stating that he or she has been sexually assaulted
- Acting like an adult, not a child

"Wouldn't I know a child abuser if I saw one?"

False assumptions we make:
- We assume it will happen to someone else.
- We assume we are safe.
- We assume we can recognize child abusers (i.e., they will be "monsters" and not like us).
- We assume child abusers exist only in certain social and economic demographics.

Profile of a Child Abuser
Abusers are often the people that you'd least expect:
- More than eighty percent of the time, the abuser is someone known to the victim. Most abuse takes place within the context of an ongoing relationship.
- A predator can be a member of a church. Some predators are known to deliberately target churches.
- The usual offender is between twenty and thirty years old.
- Some sex offenders begin their activity before the age of eighteen.
- Most are men, but there are some women.
- Predators are often married and have children.
- They come from every economic and social demographic.

How can I best minister to a child who has been abused or neglected?

As a children's ministry worker, you are an important part of the healing and redemption process for any child in your care who has been abused or neglected. It is important that you do the following:

- Pray for the children you are working with, that they will be safe, secure, and loved.
- Speak to children with integrity. Children will often feel safe in a church setting and may open up to you as someone they can trust. If a child says that he or she wants to tell you something, only if you promise not to tell anyone else, you should respond, "I want to hear what you have to say, but I can't promise that I can keep a secret." This way, if the child discloses any abuse or neglect, you can report it without betraying his or her trust.
- Remember that while children don't always tell the truth, it is our responsibility to listen and report what was stated. You may end up saving the life of a child!
- If any child has been abused, and we *do* know about it and action *is* being taken, there are a few things to remember when working with this child:
  - Don't force him or her to talk about it. Abuse is very painful, and retelling the story can be hard on the child.
  - Report to [APPROPRIATE STAFF OR CHURCH LEADER/S] each time the child brings up an incident of assault or abuse in any form. At the same time, keep in mind your responsibility to report the abuse to police or CPS.
  - Have lots of patience and understanding.
  - Show lots of love and care for the child.

What happens if a child touches *me* inappropriately?

First, think before this occurs about how you would respond. Then, if it does occur, proceed as follows:

- Remain calm. Ask yourself if this was accidental or on purpose.
- Redirect appropriately (e.g., "Sarah, please keep your hands to yourself").

- Take the child aside and explain good touch and bad touch if given the opportunity ("We do not touch areas covered by a swimming suit."). Take into account the age of the child with whom you are working. You should be able to talk about inappropriate touching with children ages three and older.
- For abused children, inappropriate touching may seem "normal." Or the child's inappropriate behavior may be to gain attention or see how the adult will respond.
- Notify [APPROPRIATE STAFF OR CHURCH LEADER/S].

How can I guard myself from accusation?

While appropriate physical contact with children can be an effective means of aiding in communication, it can also be easily misinterpreted. Here are a few simple rules to abide by to help protect yourself from accusation, whether you are serving in children's ministry or are just interacting with kids in the community:

- Always remain in open sight of other adults.
- Appropriate physical contact will vary according to the age of the child. What is appropriate for nursery children (holding, rocking, sitting in laps, diapering, assisting with the potty, etc.) will not be appropriate for school-age children.
- Follow the restroom-break guidelines outlined in the Child Protection Policy (CPP).
- Sitting on laps is only appropriate for ages zero through pre-K; it is not appropriate for older children. It is not appropriate for a man to pick up or hold a child who is older than pre-K.
- In some situations, a man will need to limit physical contact more than a woman in the same situation, especially when working with older children.

- Only touch children in "safe" areas and for brief times, with no rubbing or massaging. "Safe" areas generally include hands, arms, shoulders, upper back, or gentle pats on the top of a child's head. Never touch a child on or near any region that is considered private or personal (on any part of the body that a swimsuit covers), unless changing diapers or assisting nursery children with the potty.
- Never touch a child out of frustration or anger. Remember that the church's CPP stipulates that physical discipline is not an appropriate means of correcting someone else's child.

What do I do if I *suspect* that a child has been physically, emotionally, or sexually abused?

- *Alert* the [APPROPRIATE STAFF OR CHURCH LEADER/S]. Give all the information you have.
- *Do not* attempt to substantiate any allegations or suspicions. Let the authorities do this.
- *Do not* be afraid to report. We are responsible as a church community to comply with the law and cooperate fully with Child Protection Services (CPS) and law enforcement officials.
- *Do not* discuss the situation with anyone other than the proper authorities and the [APPROPRIATE STAFF OR CHURCH LEADER/S].
- *Do not* discuss the situation with the alleged abuser. This could compromise any investigation and could result in additional abuse, shame, etc. Again, let the authorities take care of this.

Who is required to report child abuse and neglect?

- In hearing of, witnessing, or suspecting abuse, a mandatory reporter is someone who by law *must* report it to police or Child Protective Services (CPS).
- Mandatory reporters are designated by the laws of the state in which they reside. [INSERT STATE-SPECIFIC IN-FORMATION ABOUT WHICH PROFESSIONALS ARE CONSIDERED MANDATORY REPORTERS IN YOUR STATE, like childcare professionals, law enforcement personnel, medical personnel, school teachers, etc.]. These people should contact the local CPS office or law enforcement agency where the incident reportedly occurred.
- Nonmandatory reporters should contact [APPROPRIATE STAFF OR CHURCH LEADER/S] before making any reports. They will give guidance about reporting.

How do I know if something is reportable or not?

State guidelines specify what must be reported. [INSERT STATE SPECIFIC GUIDELINES.] Typically, a report must be made when the reporter suspects or has reasons to believe that a child has been abused or neglected. Another standard frequently used is that one should report when he or she knows of or observes a child being subjected to conditions that would reasonably result in harm to the child. *For more information, contact* [APPROPRIATE STAFF OR CHURCH LEADER/S].

Training Scenarios
for Staff and Volunteers

Eighteen Scenarios for Preventing Abuse and Creating a Safe Environment at Church

1. A child of a first-time visitor starts to act out and give the teachers a very hard time. One of the teachers, Mr. Smith, is a kind, older gentleman. He removes the boy from the classroom, takes him into the hallway, briefly addresses his behavior and has him sit in a chair for a ten-minute time-out.

Questions to consider: Was it okay for Mr. Smith to take the visiting child out in the hallway for a time-out? What would you have done? What guidelines are in your CPP for this situation?

2. Two childcare workers are watching a group of four- and five-year-olds in the church nursery. One of the girls has to go to the bathroom, so the female volunteer takes her down the hallway to the girls' room; the male volunteer stays behind to watch the rest of the kids.

Questions to consider: Was it okay for the female volunteer to take the girl to the bathroom? Was it okay to leave the male volunteer alone with the children? Does your CPP have guidelines for taking children to the restroom? If so, how would those guidelines apply to this situation?

3. A child and his mother are given matching bracelets as the mother drops her son off at the children's ministry check-in desk. At the end of the service, a parent returns and says to the childcare volunteer in the classroom, "Oops, I must have lost my parent identity bracelet. Sorry about that." Feeling the awkwardness of the moment, the volunteer responds with a quick, "No worries. It happens all the time." The mother takes her son and heads home.

Questions to consider: Was it okay for the volunteer to give the child back to the parent, even if she didn't have the bracelet anymore? Would it *ever* be okay to do so? For example, what if the volunteer knew the parent really well? Depending on what your church uses for a check-in or checkout process, how would this situation be handled in your church? Does your CPP have guidelines for checking in or checking out children in your church? If so, how would those guidelines apply to this situation?

4. The children's ministry director goes around to the classrooms. As she does roll call, she realizes that one of the children is missing from the nursery. The nursery workers start to panic.

Questions to consider: What should the children's ministry director or nursery workers do in this situation? How long would it take before you contact the parents? Is there a way to lock down your building to make sure a child has not wandered off—or even worse, been taken by an abuser?

5. A child in the classroom hits another child with a toy. A childcare worker notices the incident and helps out the hurt child. There is a cut on the child's arm. After the childcare worker helps the hurt child, he decides to talk with the offending child.

Questions to consider: What should the childcare worker do to address this situation? Is there a first-aid box available in the classroom? If not, where can one be found? How should the childcare worker help the offending child realize his wrong? Should he get both children to reconcile with one another? What should the childcare worker tell the parents of both children? Does your CPP have guidelines for discipline in the classroom? What is allowed, and what is not allowed? If there are guidelines on classroom discipline in the CPP, how would those guidelines apply to this situation?

6. A child punches another child in the face and refuses to be restrained by the teachers.

Questions to consider: What should the teacher do in this situation? Is the teacher allowed to physically restrain the child so he does not do harm to the other children? How should the teacher help the hurt child? Should the teacher notify both sets of parents? Does your CPP have guidelines for uncontrollable children? If so, how would those guidelines apply to this situation?

7. Two visiting parents decide to stay with their child in the children's classroom since the new boy is having a hard time adjusting. They don't seem to be concerned about the fact that they are missing the church service.

Questions to consider: Does the CPP allow the parents to stay in the classroom for a while in order to help the child adjust? If so, how long can they stay? If they are not allowed to stay in the classroom, what should be done with their child?

8. Tom, a homeless man from the community, wanders into the children's ministry wing by mistake.

Questions to consider: Who would help Tom? Is there some form of hall monitor or security guard that can escort him to the church service? Who should the children's ministry director or volunteer contact if there is no hall monitor to help out?

9. A parent walks in with his child with a box full of cupcakes. It's his son's birthday, and he thought it would be a fun surprise for all of the kids to have a special treat.

Questions to consider: What are the food and drink guidelines for the children's classrooms? How do they apply to this situation? Can the teacher accept the cupcakes? How will the teacher know if any of the kids have food allergies? What if this was not a parent with cupcakes, but instead a teacher walking in with a cup of coffee and a snack from a donut shop for himself and the students? Would that change anything?

10. Jonathan calls the church. There are two boys in his neighborhood who play with his son and who have been coming with their family to church. He can't bring them this Sunday since they will be out of town, so he wanted to see if someone else could pick them up.

Questions to consider: What are the guidelines for transportation of children to and from the church and the home? Who is allowed to pick them up? Do you need parental consent? If something goes wrong with the kids at church, who will be responsible for them?

11. The youth are going to have a sleepover at the church building. The youth minister, plus several of the volunteers, will be with the kids.

Questions to consider: Are there guidelines in your CPP for youth sleepovers? What kind of consent is needed from the parents? What should the sleeping arrangements be? Will the kids be allowed to play outside, or must they stay in the building? What are the kids allowed to bring to the sleepover (electronic devices, games, movies, etc.)? What if this was a youth retreat at a retreat center in the mountains? How would that change things?

12. One of the volunteers for the first-grade class calls in sick at the last minute. Parents are arriving with their children, ready to check them in. There is only one adult volunteer in the classroom at this moment.

Questions to consider: Are the parents allowed to leave their children with only one volunteer present? Is there a way to contact other volunteers to ask someone to step in at the last minute? Can you ask parents to fill in? If so, which parents are allowed to help?

13. A background screening comes back with a potential volunteer having several DUIs and speeding tickets.

Questions to consider: What should the children's ministry director do in this situation? Who is responsible for deciding if this person will be allowed to work with children or not? What else would you need to know about this situation in order to make a decision?

14. A children's ministry teacher asks the teaching assistant, a twelve-year-old boy, to take a five-year-old boy to the restroom.

Questions to consider: Is this situation okay, according to your CPP? Who is allowed to take children to the restroom? Who's not allowed to do this? What is a helper allowed to do in a classroom setting? Could the teacher take the five-year-old to the restroom alone and let the twelve-year-old watch over the rest of the children in the classroom?

15. A man who is known to be a convicted sex offender shows up at the church for the Sunday service.

Questions to consider: Does your CPP specify what to do in this situation? Does he need a chaperone while at church? What if he decides to come back the next week? What would the leaders, children's ministry director, and members need to do if he wanted to join?

16. A potential children's ministry volunteer responds affirmatively on the screening application that he or she has struggled with pornography for several years.

Questions to consider: What would you do in this kind of situation? How would you minister so as to help the person fight habitual sin and grow in faith in Christ? How would such sin struggles affect the person's ability to participate in children's ministry? Would you allow him or her to be a teacher or a childcare worker? If yes, why? If no, why? What if the struggle was with same-sex attraction? What about struggles with anger? What if someone confessed to abusing a sibling as a teenager? What if the person had a sexually communicable disease, like herpes? What if he or she had been abused as a child? How would any of these problems affect your decision on whether or not to allow this person to volunteer?

17. A father arrives to pick up his five-year-old son from class; the mother had checked in the son. The volunteer teacher remembers the children's ministry director saying that the parents were separated. The father asks for his son and begins to get agitated as the volunteer hesitates.

Questions to consider: What should the volunteer do? What should he say to the father? What should the children's ministry director have told the teacher? Are there guidelines in your CPP concerning divorced or separated couples?

18. Two teenagers are caught having sex with one another on a youth retreat.

Questions to consider: What should the youth minister do? Tell someone else in the church (church leaders, parents, etc.)? Are there guidelines in your CPP for this situation, and, if so, how do they apply? What if the scenario was different and the teenagers were making out and fondling one another (and no clothes were removed)?

10 Scenarios for Responding to Abuse

1. While changing diapers, a childcare worker notices bruises on a child's backside.

Questions to consider: Who should this worker tell? Is there a clearly designated contact person in the church for reporting abuse? Is the childcare worker no longer obligated to deal with this situation after explaining it to the contact person? Does the worker still have a duty to report the abuse to police or CPS? What should the childcare worker do if the church tells him or her to not report anything to police or CPS? How do certain medical conditions that cause or are associated with skin discolorations (such as Mongolian spot) pertain to this scenario?

2. A child comments in class to one of his teachers that his dad drinks a lot, gets very angry, and sometimes hits him or his sisters.

Questions to consider: What should this teacher say to the child? Whom should this teacher tell? Is there a clearly designated contact person in the church for reporting abuse? Is the teacher obligated to deal with this situation after explaining it to the contact person? Does the teacher still have a duty to report the abuse to police or CPS? What are the state guidelines for reporting? What if the church decides not to say anything? Would this situation be any different if the teacher were a mandatory reporter?

3. A parent finds out that his daughter has been romantically involved with the youth minister for a number of months. He calls the pastor to talk about the troubling news.

Questions to consider: What should this pastor do? Is there anyone else in the church who should know? Should the pastor confront the youth minister or interview the daughter? Is there a clear contact person in the church for reporting abuse? Does the pastor have a duty to report the abuse to police or CPS? What if the parents don't want to report it? What if the girl refuses to talk about the abuse to the pastor or the police? What if this was an anonymous tip? Would that change anything?

4. A pastor at Faith Church calls a pastor at Grace Church and says that their former youth director was reported to have sent inappropriate texts to teenagers in the youth group. The pastor doesn't have any details about the actual texts, apart from saying that the parents are very upset. This youth director has been working for Grace Church for two years.

Questions to consider: Should the pastor at Grace Church look into the allegations any further or confront the youth director? Does the leadership of the church or the youth's parents need to know? Should the pastor share this information with anyone else? Does the CPP offer any guidelines on what to do in this situation?

5. The director of the children's choir rapes one of the teenagers in the church. The story comes out about a year after it happened.

Questions to consider: How should the church care for the victim? How should the church deal with the director of the children's choir? How and when should the leaders communicate with the congregation? How should the church discipline the man? Should they ask him to find a different church if the victim is still in attendance? Should the church contact the media? If so, how and when should the leaders say something to the media? Does your CPP offer any guidelines on what to do in this situation? If so, how do these guidelines apply?

6. A man who grew up in your church and moved away several years ago calls the current pastor and says he was abused by a former Sunday school teacher.

Questions to consider: How should the pastor handle this situation? How should the church respond to these allegations? When should the pastor contact the church's lawyers or insurance company?

Should the church handle this situation by themselves? Should they hire an outside investigator? Should the leaders report the allegations to the congregation? If so, how and when should the leaders communicate with the congregation? Should the leaders say something to the media? If so, how and when should the leaders say something to the media? Does your CPP offer any guidelines on what to do in this situation? If so, how do those guidelines apply?

7. A man who is a member of your church is caught molesting kids in his neighborhood. You discover this through local news reports.

Questions to consider: How should the church handle this situation? Should the church confront the alleged perpetrator? Should the church contact the police and CPS to get more information? When should the church seek out legal counsel? Should the church discipline this man? Which biblical texts (Matthew 18; 1 Corinthians 5; or 2 Corinthians 2) are most relevant to this situation? How and when should the church leadership communicate with the congregation? How and when should the leadership make contact with the media? What would you need to do if this man was involved in children's ministry in your church? Does your CPP offer any guidelines on what to do in this situation? If so, how do those guidelines apply?

8. Two parents come to the youth minister concerned that their son's female youth sponsor seems overly interested in spending time alone with him. They are trying to discern if they are overreacting.

Questions to consider: What should the youth minister do? Speak to the female youth sponsor and/or to the son? Should the youth minister tell anyone else in the church? Are there guidelines in the CPP for this situation, and, if so, how do they apply? If the female youth sponsor were a college student, how would that affect the situation? Should college students be allowed to help out with the youth group?

9. A nineteen-year-old college student comes to the pastor and shares that when she was about six years old, a fifteen-year-old girl in her neighborhood had played "doctor" with her. She thinks she was abused but is not sure because she's suppressed the memories for so long.

Questions to consider: What should the pastor say to this woman? How should the pastor bring comfort and hope to her? What if this woman still regularly encountered this person? How would that affect the situation? Should the pastor enlist the help of a counselor? If the pastor looks for a counselor, what qualities is the pastor looking for in a counselor? Should this woman enlist the pastor's help or the help of a godly older woman in the church? What if the scenario were different and the fifteen-year-old were a boy playing "doctor" with a six-year-old girl? How would that change this situation and your responses? Or if the victim were now forty-five years old and had been abused as a six-year-old, how would that affect the situation?

10. A college student who helps out with the youth group is caught having sex with one of the high school students.

Questions to consider: What should the youth minister do? Tell someone else in the church (church leaders, parents, etc.)? Are there guidelines in your CPP for this situation, and, if so, how do they apply? Should college students be allowed to help out with the youth group? What if the scenario was different and the students were making out and fondling one another (and no clothes were removed)?

Endnotes

Chapter 1: The Nature of the Problem

1. I got the idea for this introduction from Cornelius Plantinga's brilliant work, *Not the Way It Is Supposed to Be: A Breviary of Sin* (Grand Rapids, MI: Eerdmans, 1995), 7.

2. "Sex Offender Statistics," Statistic Brain, accessed February 11, 2014, http://www.statisticbrain.com/sex-offender-statistics.

3. Robin Sax, *Predators and Child Molesters: What Every Parent Needs to Know to Keep Kids Safe* (Amherst, NY: Prometheus, 2009), 24–25.

4. The U.S. Department of Justice NSOPW (National Sexual Offender Public Website), accessed February 11, 2014, http://www.nsopr.gov/en/Education/FactsMythsStatistics#reference.

5. Ibid.

6. Ibid.

7. Ibid.

8. U.S. Department of Justice Bureau of Statistics, "Sexual Assault of Young Children as Reported to Law Enforcement: Victim, Incident, and Offender Characteristics," 10, accessed February 11, 2014, http://www.bjs.gov/content/pub/pdf/saycrle.pdf.

9. Ibid., 2, accessed February 11, 2014, http://www.bjs.gov/content/pub/pdf/saycrle.pdf.

10. Boz Tchividjian, "Startling Statistics: Child sexual abuse and what the church can begin doing about it," RNS: Religion News Service, accessed February 11, 2014, http://boz.religionnews.com/2014/01/09/startling-statistics/.

11. Sax, *Predators and Child Molesters*, 24–25.

12. Anna Salter, *Predators: Pedophiles, Rapists, and Other Sex Offenders: Who They Are, How They Operate, and How We Can Protect Ourselves and Our Children* (New York: Pereus, 2003), 36–37.

13. Ibid., 37.

Chapter 3: The False Assumptions We Make

14. Andrew Schmutzer, ed., *The Long Journey Home: Understanding and Ministering to the Sexually Abused* (Eugene, OR: Wipf & Stock, 2011), 44.

15. Carla van Dam, *Identifying Child Molesters: Preventing Child Sexual Abuse by Recognizing the Patterns of the Offenders* (New York: The Haworth Maltreatment and Trauma Press, 2001), 81.

Chapter 4: Types, Techniques, and Targets of Sexual Predators

1. Gavin de Becker, forward to Salter, *Predators*, xi.

2. Ibid.

3. Jaycee Dugard, *A Stolen Life: A Memoir* (New York: Simon & Schuster, 2011), 9–11. See also Barbara Walters' very sobering video interview of Jaycee online: accessed February 5, 2014, www.abcnews.go.com/US/jaycee_dugard/.

4. Ibid.

5. Boz Tchividjian, "5 Things You Should Know about Child Sexual Offenders," Resurgence, accessed February 14, 2014, http://theresurgence. com/2012/04/14/5-things-you-should-know-about-child-sexual-offenders. The study Tchividjian cites is the Abel and Harlow Child Molestation Prevention Study (2002), accessed December 1, 2013, http://www.child molestationprevention.org/pages/study.html. This study further states, "Of the 3,952 men who admitted to being child molesters, 68 percent reported that they had molested a child in their family" (8). For a more in-depth look, see Gene Abel and Nora Harlow, *The Stop Child Molestation Book* (Bloomington, IN: Xlibris, 2001).

6. James Cobble, Richard Hammer, and Steven Klipowicz, *Reducing the Risk II: Making Your Church Safe From Sexual Abuse* (Carol Stream, IL: Church Law & Tax Report, 2003), 12.

7. Salter, *Predators*, 76–78. The Abel and Harlow Child Molestation Prevention Study gives a sense of how many men versus women are molesters: "Of a sample of 4,007 men and women who admit to molesting a child 13 years old or younger, 99 percent were male and 1 percent were female" (8).

8. Ibid., 38.

9. Victor Vieth, "What Would Walther Do? Applying the Law and Gospel to Victims and Perpetrators of Child Sexual Abuse," *Journal of Psychology & Theology* 40, no. 4 (2012): 263.

10. Salter, *Predators*, 42.

11. Van Dam, *Identifying Child Molesters*, 110–112.

12. Ibid. This scenario is based on Van Dam's case study two, "Mr. Clay," and has been adjusted to fit a church context, 16–25. Sexual abuse does happen at the hands of Sunday School teachers; see also Britt Johnsen,

"Sunday School Teacher Pleads Guilty to Criminal Sex Charge," *Winona Daily News*, accessed December 1, 2013, http://www.winonadailynews.com/news/article_7492e940-986d-55ce-8c8d-9513de50e9fd.html.

13. Vieth, "What Would Walther Do?", 263.

14. Van Dam, *Identifying Child Molesters*, 104.

15. Jeff Brady, "'Who Would Believe a Kid?' The Sandusky Jury," NPR, accessed October 23, 2012, http://www.npr.org/2012/06/23/155621728/sandusky-verdict-answers-who-would-believe-a-kid.

16. Salter, *Predators*, 43.

17. Van Dam, *Identifying Child Molesters*, 77.

18. Victor Vieth, "Suffer the Children: Developing Effective Church Policies on Child Maltreatment," *Jacob's Hope: A Newsletter of the Jacob Wetterling Resource Center* 2, no. 1 (June 2011), 2.

19. Vieth, "What Would Walther Do?", 263.

20. Salter, *Predators*, 199.

Chapter 5: Why the Church?

1.   You can read the full account of Christa Brown's life in her book, *This Little Light: Beyond a Baptist Preacher Predator and His Gang* (Cedarburg, WI: Foremost), 2009.

2.   Salter, *Predators*, 28.

3.   Ibid., 29.

4.   Boz Tchividjian, *Protecting Children from Abuse in the Church: Steps to Prevent and Respond* (Greensboro, NC: New Growth, 2013), 12.

5.   Kelly Clark, "Institutional Child Sexual Abuse—Not Just a Catholic Thing," *William Mitchell Law Review* 36, no. 1 (2009–10): 232.

6.   Boz Tchividjian, "Offenders in the Church: Who are they and how do they operate?" (video), accessed November 15, 2013, http://vimeo.com/58304996.

7.   Laurie Goodstein, "Vatican Decline to Defrock U.S. Priest Who Abused Boys," *The New York Times*, March 26, 2010, http://www.nytimes.com/2010/03/25/world/europe/25vatican.html.; Ibid., "For Years, Deaf Boys Tried to Tell of Priest's Abuse," *The New York Times*, March 26, 2010, http://www.nytimes.com/2010/03/27/us/27wisconsin.html.; Ibid., "Exiled Pedophile Priest May Have Continued Abuse," *New York Times*, April 2, 2010, http://www.nytimes.com/2010/04/03/us/03wisconsin.html.

8.   Clark, "Institutional Child Sexual Abuse—Not Just a Catholic Thing," 232.

9.   Tchividjian, *Protecting Children from Abuse in the Church*, 8–10.

10. Vieth, "What Would Walther Do?", 270–71.

Chapter 6: Creating and Implementing a Child Protection Policy

1. Capitol Hill Baptist Church, "Child Protection Policy," November 2013, 8. http://www.capitolhillbaptist.org/wp-content/uploads/ChildProtectionPolicy.pdf

2. Sojourn Community Church, SojournKids basic training manual, October 2011, 11.

3. Cobble, Hammer, and Klipowicz, *Reducing the Risk II*, 42–44.

4. Ibid., 41–44.

5. Beth Swagman, *Preventing Child Abuse: Creating a Safe Place* (Grand Rapids, MI: Faith Alive Christian Resources, 2009), 9.

6. Cobble, Hammer, and Klipowicz, *Reducing the Risk II*, 40–41.

7. Ibid., 42.

8. Ibid., 40.

9. Swagman, *Preventing Child Abuse*, 20–21.

10. Cobble, Hammer, and Klipowicz, *Reducing the Risk II*, 40.

11. Swagman, *Preventing Child Abuse*, 9–11.

Chapter 7: A Check-in and Checkout Process

1. Sojourn Community Church, SojournKids basic training manual, October 2011, 11.

Chapter 8: Membership

1. Cobble, Hammer, and Klipowicz, *Reducing the Risk II*, 25–26.

2. Jared Wilson, "Safeguarding Against Abuse in the Church," The Gospel Coalition, accessed February 5, 2014, http://thegospelcoalition.org/blogs/gospeldrivenchurch/2012/12/13/safeguarding-against-abuse-in-the-church.

3. Jonathan Leeman, *Church Membership: How The World Knows Who Represents Jesus* (Wheaton, IL: Crossway, 2012), 26–27, 51.

4. Salter, *Predators*, 225.

Chapter 9: Screening and Verification

1. Salter, *Predators*, 196.

2. Cobble, Hammer, and Klipowicz, *Reducing the Risk II*, 32.

3. Ibid., 26.

4. Swagman, *Preventing Child Abuse*, 53.

5. Ibid., 54.

6. Cobble, Hammer, and Klipowicz, *Reducing the Risk II*, 27; see also Swagman, *Preventing Child Abuse*, 31.

7. Swagman, *Preventing Child Abuse*, 52.

8. Vieth, "Suffer the Children," 4.

9. Ibid.

10. Salter, *Predators*, 227.

11. Vieth, "Suffer the Children," 4.

12. Cobble, Hammer, and Klipowicz, *Reducing the Risk II*, 34.

13. Ibid., 35.

14. Ibid., 28.

15. Swagman, *Preventing Child Abuse*, 55.

16. Cobble, Hammer, and Klipowicz, *Reducing the Risk II*, 25.

17. Swagman, *Preventing Child Abuse*, 55.

18. Ibid., 56.

19. Ibid., 57; see also Cobble, Hammer, and Klipowicz, *Reducing the Risk II*, 33.

20. Wilson, "Safeguarding against Abuse in the Church."

21. Cobble, Hammer, and Klipowicz, *Reducing the Risk II*, 19.

22. Ibid., 20.

23. Ibid., 24.

24. Salter, *Predators,* 196.

25. Sarah Burge, "Religion: No Law on Church Worker Checks," *The Press-Enterprise*, May 31, 2011, http://www.pe.com/local-news/riverside-county/murrieta/murrieta-headlines-index/20110531-religion-no-law-on-church-worker-checks.ece.

Chapter 12: Preparing Church Leaders, Parents, Children, and Teens *Before* Abuse Happens

1. Wilson, "Safeguarding against Abuse in the Church."

2. Ibid.

3. Tchividjian, *Protecting Children from Abuse in the Church*, 23.

4. Vieth, "Suffer the Children," 4.

5. Boz Tchividjian and Victor Vieth, "When the Child Abuser Has a Bible: Investigating Child Maltreatment Sanctioned or Condoned by a Religious Leader," *Centerpiece* 2, no. 12 (2010): 3.

Chapter 13: Getting to Know the People and Resources in Your Community

1. Wilson, "Safeguarding against Abuse at Church."

2. Vieth, "Suffer the Children," 4.

3. Ibid.

4. L. Martin Nussbaum and Theresa Lynn Sidebotham, "Are Protestant Ministries a New Market? Lessons Learned from the Catholic Scandal," accessed February 5, 2014, http://www.rothgerber.com/files/10368_Are ProtestantMinistriesaNewMarket.pdf.

5. Vieth, "Suffer the Children," 4. For further reading, see Mike Johnson, "The Investigative Windows of Opportunity: The Vital Link to Corroboration in Child Sexual Abuse Cases," *Centerpiece* 1, no. 9 (2009), http://www.gundersenhealth.org/upload/docs/NCPTC/CenterPiece/Vol%20 1%20Issue%209.pdf.

6. Tamara Hurst, "Prevention of Recantations of Child Sexual Abuse Cases," *Centerpiece* 2, no. 11 (2010), http://www.gundersenhealth.org/upload/ docs/NCPTC/Jacobs-Hope/Jacobs-Hope-vol2-issue1.pdf.

7. Vieth, "Suffer the Children," 4.

8. For a complete listing of clergy reporting laws, see U.S. Department of Health and Human Services, "Clergy as Mandatory Reporters of Child Abuse and Neglect," accessed December 1, 2013, https://www.childwelfare. gov/systemwide/laws_policies/statutes/clergymandated.pdf.

9. Vieth, "Suffer the Children," 4.

10. Thanks to pastor and author Jonathan Leeman, who helped me think through these texts. I've essentially summarized our correspondence via email from November 2013.

Chapter 14: Helping a Church to Be Responsible by Reporting Child Abuse

1. Robert Bergen, *1, 2 Samuel*, vol. 7, *The New American Commentary*, gen. ed. E. Ray Clendenen (Nashville: Broadman & Holman, 1996), 383. Some scholars debate whether David could have made Amnon marry Tamar since the law also prohibited close kinsmen from marrying each other (Leviticus 18:11; 20:17).

2. Joyce Baldwin, *1 and 2 Samuel*, *Tyndale Old Testament Commentaries* (Downers Grove, IL: InterVarsity Press, 2008), 267. Baldwin notes that the Septuagint (LXX) indicates David reacted to the outrage with anger, "but he would not hurt Amnon because he was his eldest son and he loved him."

3. Study notes to *The English Standard Version Study Bible* (Wheaton, IL: Crossway, 2008), 563.

4. U.S. Department of Health and Human Services, "Child Maltreatment 2011," 19, www.acf.hhs.gov/sites/default/files/cb/cm11.pdf.

5. Ibid., 70.

6. Pat Wingert, "Priests Commit No More Abuse Than Other Males," *Newsweek*, April 8, 2010, http://www.newsweek.com/priests-commit-no-more-abuse-other-males-70625.

7. Victor Vieth et al., "Lessons from Penn State: A Call To Implement a New Pattern of Training for Mandated Reporters and Child Protection Professionals," *Centerpiece* 3, nos. 3 and 4 (2012), http://www.gundersenhealth. org/upload/docs/NCPTC/CenterPiece/Vol_3_Issue_3__4.pdf.

8. For the remainder of this chapter, I've leaned very heavily on Swagman, *Preventing Child Abuse*, 61–73, and Cobble, Hammer, and Klipowicz, *Reducing the Risk II*, 52–54.

9. U.S. Department of Health and Human Services Administration for Children and Families, "Mandated Reporting," Child Welfare Information Gateway, accessed February 5, 2014, www.childwelfare.gov/responding/ mandated.cfm. This site contains more information about the state-by-state regulations on mandatory reporting, including those for clergy.

10. Swagman, *Preventing Child Abuse*, 62.

11. Ibid., 63.

12. Vieth and Tchividjian, "When the Child Abuser Has a Bible," 3.

13. The Commission on Theology and Church Relations of the Lutheran Church—Missouri Synod, *The Pastor-Penitent Relationship: Privileged Communications* (1999), 12.

14. Ibid., 14. The pertinent passage here is the following: "A communication made by a penitent seeking absolution for a particular act must not be divulged, even if the act was criminal and even if the law may compel its disclosure. We recognize that in such an instance, the pastor's refusal may lead to criminal prosecution while his disclosure may lead to church discipline."

15. Cobble, Hammer, and Klipowicz, *Reducing the Risk II*, 54.

16. Swagman, *Preventing Child Abuse*, 70.

17. Ibid., 65.

18. Ibid., 66.

19. Marie Rhode, "Assault Victim Sues School Synod," *Milwaukee Journal Sentinel*, May 8, 2008, http://www.jsonline.com/news/education/ 29529999.html; quoted in Vieth, "Suffer the Children," 5.

20. Swagman, *Preventing Child Abuse*, 69.

21. Ibid., 65.

22. Ibid., 66.

23. Cobble, Hammer, and Klipowicz, *Reducing the Risk II*, 53.

24. Ibid., 54.

Chapter 15: Helping a Church to Respond Wisely to Victims, the Congregation, and the Media

1. Peter Eisler, "Church Abuse Cases and Lawyers an Uneasy Mix," *USA Today*, May 10, 2011, http://usatoday30.usatoday.com/news/religion/2011- 05-09-vienna-virginia-church-abuse-case-lawyers-insurers_n.htm; Josh White, "Vienna Presbyterian Church Seeks Forgiveness, Redemption in the Wake of

Abuse Scandal," *Washington Post*, April 2, 2011, http://www.washingtonpost. com/local/vienna-presbyterian-church-works-to-overcome-revelations-of-sexual-abuse/2011/03/30/AF3hNxQC_story.html.

2.   White, "Vienna Presbyterian Church Seeks Forgiveness, Redemption in the Wake of Abuse Scandal."

3.   Eisler, "Church Abuse Cases and Lawyers an Uneasy Mix."

4.   Ibid.

5.   Ibid.

6.   Clark, "Institutional Child Sexual Abuse—Not Just a Catholic Thing," 235.

7.   Eisler, "Church Abuse Cases and Lawyers an Uneasy Mix."

8.   White, "Vienna Presbyterian Church Seeks Forgiveness, Redemption in the Wake of Abuse Scandal."

9.   Diane Langberg, *Counseling Survivors of Sexual Abuse* (Maitland, FL: Xulon, 2003), 87–90.

10. Boz Tchividjian, "When Faith Hurts: How the Christian Community Can Serve Survivors of Sexual Abuse" (video), accessed February 24, 2014, http://vimeo.com/60270235.

11. Vieth, "What Would Walther Do?", 267.

12. Ibid.

13. Ibid.

14. Ibid., 268.

15. Tchividjian, "When Faith Hurts."

16. Ibid.

17. Clark, "Institutional Child Sexual Abuse—Not Just a Catholic Thing," 235–239.

18. Ibid., 233.

19. Ibid., 233–234.

20. Cobble, Hammer, and Klipowicz, *Reducing the Risk II*, 59.

21. Ibid., 60.

22. Ibid., 60.

23. Bill Anderson, *When Child Abuse Comes to Church: For Parents, Church Leaders, and Anyone Who Provides Care for Children* (Minneapolis: Bethany, 1992), 72.

24. Swagman, *Preventing Child Abuse*, 83.

25. Ibid., 83–84.

26. Anderson, 71–72.

Chapter 16: Helping a Church to Deal Wisely with a Child Abuser

1.   Vieth, "Suffer the Children," 5; Vieth, "What Would Walther Do?", 270–271.

2. Vieth, "Suffer the Children," 5.

3. Wilson, "Safeguarding Against Abuse in the Church."

4. Denise George, "What Forgiveness Isnt [sic]," G.R.A.C.E., accessed February 5, 2014, http://netgrace.org/wp-content/uploads/What-Forgiveness-Isnt1.pdf.

5. Vieth, "What Would Walther Do?", 271.

6. Vieth, "Suffer the Children," 5.

7. Ibid.

8. Ibid.

9. Vieth, "What Would Walther Do?", 264.

10. Cobble, Hammer, and Klipowicz, *Reducing the Risk II*, 57–59.

11. United States Conference of Catholic Bishops, "Charter for the Protection of Children and Young People," Article 5 (June 16, 2011), http://www.usccb.org/issues-and-action/child-and-youth-protection/charter.cfm.

12. Nussbaum and Sidebotham, "Are Protestant Ministries a New Market?", 15.

13. Ibid., 14.

Appendix A: A Really Quick Guide to Writing and Implementing a Child Protection Policy

1. Swagman, *Preventing Child Abuse*, 17.

2. Cobble, Hammer, and Klipowicz, *Reducing the Risk II*, 67–71.

Appendix B: Child-on-Child Sexual Abuse

1. U.S. Department of Health and Human Services, "Child Maltreatment 2011," 68.

2. Jane Silvosky and Barbara Bonner, "Sexual Development and Sexual Behavior Problems in Children 2–12," *The Newsletter for the National Center for Sexual Behavior for Youth*, 4 (January 2004): 1–4.

3. Cobble, Hammer, and Klipowicz, *Reducing the Risk II*, 45.

4. Joy Melton, *Safe Sanctuaries: Reducing the Risk of Abuse in the Church for Children and Youth* (Nashville: Discipleship Resources, 2012), 86–87.

Appendix C: How Do I Talk to My Kids about Sexual Abuse?

1. Darkness to Light, "More Tips for Talking with Children about Sexual Abuse," accessed March 6, 2014, http://www.d2l.org/site/c.4dICIJOkGcISE/b.8044377/k.FD58/More_Tips_for_Talking_with_Children_About_Sexual_Abuse.htm.

Appendix E: Child Abuse and Neglect Training Sheet

1.   Adapted from a training sheet used at Sojourn Community Church, Lexington, KY. Used with permission. Feel free to adapt this for your own context so that you can train staff and volunteers in your children's ministry.